LIVING WITH YOUR PASSIONS

LIVING WITH YOUR PASSIONS

ERWIN W. LUTZER

While this book is designed for the reader's personal enjoyment and profit, it is also intended for group study. A Leader's Guide with Victor Multiuse Transparency Masters is available from your local bookstore or from the publisher.

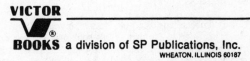

VICTOR BOOKS a division of SP Publications, Inc.
WHEATON. ILLINOIS 60187

Offices also in
Whitby. Ontario. Canada
Amersham-on-the-Hill. Bucks. England

Third printing, 1985

Most of the Scripture quotations in this book are from the
New American Standard Bible (NASB), © the Lockman Foundation
1960, 1962, 1963, 1968, 1971, 1972, 1973, 1975, 1977. Other quotations
are from the *King James Version* (KJV); the *Holy Bible, New International Version* (NIV), © 1973, 1978, 1984, International Bible Society.
Used by permission of Zonderan Bible Publishers; and *The Living Bible*
(TLB), © 1971, Tyndale House Publishers, Wheaton, IL 60189. Used by
permission.

Recommended Dewey Decimal Classification: 248.27

Suggested Subject Headings: CHRISTIAN LIFE: SPIRITUAL DISCIPLINES

Library of Congress Catalog Card Number: 83-60817
ISBN: 0-88207-294-3

Contents

Foreword

Listen to voices in our society and you'll believe that the passport to happiness is sexual permissiveness. The bumper sticker "If it feels good, do it!" is for many the moral principle to govern actions.

Millions are caught up in the elusive pursuit of pleasure: one-night sexual liaisons, pornography, and drugs. These, with all their tantalizing promises, are supposed to make us healthier and happier people.

Do they?

God established physical laws—gravity, for instance. He also ordained spiritual laws. When we break them there are built-in consequences. Whatever we sow, we reap; in fact, we always reap more than we sow, though we may not be aware of it immediately because the harvest comes much later. Still our passions won't listen to careful reasoning. They scream for fulfillment, *whatever the price.*

You'll soon learn that this author as a counselor has heard all the rationalizations that accompany sexual sin. He's listened to the familiar cry, "I know what I should do, but I can't!"

Is there a way out?

This book offers hope. Our passions are powerful. Our sexual desires do burn out of control, but there is freedom found in submitting to Jesus Christ.

This book points us to the pathway to true freedom and to victory. The Word of God through the Holy Spirit is able to tear down the strongholds of the imagination. Though the commands of the New Testament seem impossible, God gives us the ability to do what we should. Though temptation is ever with us, freedom from the tyranny of passions is not an idle dream.

The author faces issues that are often conveniently overlooked by evangelical ministers. Masturbation, homosexuality, and demonic warfare are treated biblically and with sensitivity. He urges putting our pasts behind and stresses the need for emotional wholeness.

The book is characterized by its practical insights into the temptations and frustrations of sexual passion. The subtle influences of the world are exposed.

I'm glad to recommend this book to the Christian public.

JOSH MCDOWELL
Julian, California

1

The Battle with
Passions

"I got saved six months ago, but nobody told my glands!" Most of us identify with this 18-year-old, in a conflict as old as the human race: the struggle of sexual feelings against the restraints of conscience and the teachings of the Bible. Our passions cry *yes* when our better moral judgment cries *no*!

On the one hand the teachings of the New Testament warn against sexual promiscuity (1 Cor. 6:18). Christ taught that everyone who looks at another with lust has already committed adultery inwardly (Matt. 5:28). This precept, and others Jesus taught, conflict with the strong sexual desires that tantalize so many of us, especially men. How can we obey God's teachings when our sexual urges feel so right, so proper, so beautiful?

One Christian man who was overcome by sexual temptation bought a pornographic magazine. When his lust was satisfied, he was so disgusted with himself that he burned the magazine in the bathroom sink. Yet an hour later he was back sifting through the ashes, hoping to find some erotic pictures which had escaped the flames! Such is the dilemma of sexual misconduct: its victims alternate between exhilaration and disgust.

How do we handle the conflict? Some surrender to the pressures of their sexual appetite. They choose the steep and attractive path of moral laxity. Believing they are free to stop at any point along the decline, they take that first step; if there are no immediate negative consequences, they continue, not knowing that well-concealed pitfalls await them along the way.

It may begin with pornography, "making out" on a date, or experiencing the exhilaration of sexual attraction toward someone other than one's own spouse. How the first step is taken makes little difference. The point is that in taking this first step downward these people are no longer taking advantage of God's restraints. They are in enemy territory, though they may not know it at this point. Perhaps years will pass before they realize that God's restrictions were for their own good. Meanwhile the scenery on the far side of the hill is too captivating; there's no time to contemplate the possible effects of their actions. In fact, no consequences in an uncertain future could possibly diminish the exhilaration of the moment.

On the Slippery Slope

Among those who have wandered off on their own and fallen on the slippery downward slope are at least two distinct groups. In one group are those who are enjoying themselves and who have no thought of returning to solid ground. Christians or not, they've decided that they know better than God; they will chart their own course without benefit of the signposts they have chosen to ignore. They naively believe that they can control the consequences of their actions—they have found a better way. Even when they suspect they are wrong, they stubbornly refuse to admit it. Better to live with emptiness and guilt; better to be spiritually bankrupt than to acknowledge a need and humbly return to God for forgiveness and moral direction.

Evangelist Juan Carlos Ortiz says that the world is like a ship that is going to sink in the deepest ocean. When the captain knows the ship is sinking, he says to the passengers: "Those of you who are in second class may pass to first class without paying. Drink all the whiskey you want—everything is free. If you want to break the lamps or smash the furniture, do it!" The passengers are impressed with the broad-mindedness of their captain. Why wouldn't they want to obey him? They've got all the freedom they want—anything they desire. On a sinking ship anything is permissible.

Many today are enjoying a sensual life without admitting that their "ship" is on the way down. Preoccupation with pleasure has long since deadened their spiritual perception. Like the children of Lot, they heed warnings with scorn and take them as jokes (Gen. 19:14), but their "ship" is sinking, and God will write the final chapter of their lives. Their eventual judgment is inevitable.

In the other group are those who have wandered into moral quicksand and would like to return to the gracious forgiveness and deliverance that God can give them. They have fallen; they've become soiled, and their consciences are constant reminders of their disobedience. A man has seduced another man's wife; a boy has been introduced to homosexuality by a friend; a beautiful 16-year-old must admit to her parents that she is pregnant, and a young woman carries with her the secret that she had an abortion.

What all these persons have in common is a desire for a new beginning. They'd like to put their past behind them. They wish they had trusted God rather than their own judgment, but they don't know how to begin. They've tried to stand up—God knows they have—but they've fallen again and again. They are almost ready to give up. They need to be encouraged and to realize they can be freed from repeated failures. The consequences of their actions may never change, but *they* can change. More accurately, God can change them!

Obeying the Warning Signals

Others have heeded the counsel of Scripture, and intend to live within the boundaries of God's will. They don't commit adultery, attend sensual movies, or make passes at their secretaries. Fortunately, they have not had to endure the shame and guilt associated with sexual misbehavior. If they don't know it already, someday they will discover that they have taken the best path. But among them are those who feel frustrated, and cheated. They feel like the elder brother who stayed to help his father build a farm. They envy those of the younger generation who have experienced the pleasure of sexual promiscuity. At times they wish they could throw caution to the wind. If they ever got away to New York where no one knows them, they might attend an X-rated movie, buy some pornography, and make up for what they've been missing. Perhaps they feel the church, or for that matter God, has not been fair with them. They've missed some thrills. For now however, perhaps because of fear, they remain within the bounds of an acceptable moral code. Yet they stand on tiptoe, trying to satisfy their curiosity and wondering what it is like on the other side. They still have to learn that God has not cheated them; they need not envy the wicked, and most importantly, it is possible to be satisfied within the prescribed limits. For those who are single, this means sexual abstinence. They will be denied the pleasure of intimate companionship and sexual love. They will learn that even this—painful though it may be for some—is better than the attractive and grossly overrated alternatives. Those who are married must also learn the same lesson, for diverse sexual attractions come to all. Marriage is not a guarantee that sexual desires will be satisfied.

Though chastity for the unmarried and fidelity for the married are not popular, such commitments are not only right, but they are best. Many believe this in their heads, but not in their hearts.

Others, probably more than we might suspect, live chaste lives, and they are satisfied. Of course they experience temptations—even powerful temptations—but they are convinced that God has their best interests in mind. They have chosen to follow obediently and are not hankering for forbidden pleasures. For them, the satisfaction of walking with God and having a clear conscience is ample reward for their obedience.

Then there are people who have in the past slipped and fallen, but they have accepted God's forgiveness. Paul wrote to the Corinthians: "Do you not know that the unrighteous shall not inherit the kingdom of God? Do not be deceived; neither fornicators, nor idolaters, nor adulterers, nor effeminate, nor homosexuals, nor thieves, nor the covetous, nor drunkards, nor revilers, nor swindlers, shall inherit the kingdom of God" (1 Cor. 6:9–10). Yet Paul continues: "*And such were some of you; but you were washed, but you were sanctified, but you were justified in the name of the Lord Jesus Christ,* and in the Spirit of our God" (6:11, italics added). Here is ample proof that God can deliver us from all kinds of sexual misconduct. Habits of the past can be broken and new patterns established. If not, Christ's power must be seriously questioned. Thousands of Christians have been freed from the tyranny of their passions. The battle never subsides; the temptation will always be there regardless of how long we have walked with God. Yet we read, "Now those who belong to Christ Jesus have crucified the flesh with its passions and desires" (Gal. 5:24). These promises provide an adequate basis for bringing our passions under the control of the Holy Spirit.

Why This Book?
For nearly two years I debated whether to write this book. First, it involves some risks. A friend who teaches marriage seminars said that whatever topic he dealt with on Sunday, he struggled with the next week. Satan, the enemy of our souls,

would like to destroy us in areas where we are trying to help God's people. I'm not immune from sexual temptation. Paul warned, "Therefore let him who thinks he stands take heed lest he fall" (1 Cor. 10:12). The apostle was deeply concerned about the possibility of stumbling as he ran the course of life. In stressing the need for self-control he wrote, "I buffet my body and make it my slave, lest possibly, after I have preached to others, I myself should be disqualified" (1 Cor. 9:27). Only the dead are beyond the possibility of sexual misbehavior.

Second, I do not claim to be an expert in counseling those who battle with passions. I've lived long enough to realize that there is no formula for victory. We cannot expect to have all emotional and sexual problems resolved by reading a book. We are involved in a battle, and that means we must be constantly alert for new strategies both in defense and offense. Superficial guidelines for victory only cause further discouragement which in turn leads to unbelief and the hopeless feeling, "That's the way I am . . . there's no hope for me." The purpose of this book is to map out a general battle strategy to help keep us from enslavement to our passions.

Third, I've become thoroughly convinced that the Bible's teaching on sex is for our own good. We all know that sensual pleasure makes incredibly attractive promises. Our passions cry for spontaneous and uninhibited expression, without a hint of any possible negative side effects. In a moment of sexual ecstasy who cares about what the church or even God has to say! But when the dust settles and all the results are in; when the guilt and shame have been considered; when the consequences in this life and in the life to come have been thoughtfully calculated, God's way will prove to be the wisest and the best. The question is whether we have the faith to act on this premise without thinking as Eve did, that we've got to "try it for ourselves."

Finally, I do believe that deliverance from sexual misbehavior is possible. Oswald Chambers wrote, "If Jesus Christ cannot deliver from sin, if He cannot adjust us perfectly to God as He says He can, if He cannot fill us with the Holy Ghost until there is nothing that can ever appeal again in sin or the world or the flesh, then He has misled us" (*God's Workmanship,* Christian Literature Crusade, p. 24). He's not talking about becoming sinless. He is saying that if Christ cannot deliver us, He has deceived us. I've known people who were freed from promiscuity, pornography, and homosexuality.

For a time Christ may allow our passions to dominate us. He wants to teach us to recognize our weaknesses, our unbelievable penchant for self-justification and rationalization. In the end, however, we can prove Him to be the deliverer He claims to be.

How serious are we in letting God give us self-control over our passions? Like Gideon, we've got to separate the casual soldier from the committed one. So here's the test: Begin by memorizing Colossians 3:1–11 ("If then you have been raised up with Christ, keep seeking the things above. . . .") and don't be satisfied until you know the passage so well you needn't even think about the mechanics. Then you can concentrate on its meaning. Jesus said, "If you abide in My Word, then you are truly disciples of Mine; and you shall know the truth, and the truth shall make you free" (John 8:31–32).

Ready for the challenge?

Study and Application

1. What factors in our society have contributed to the widespread feeling that sex should be enjoyed apart from commitment and responsibility?

2. John taught that the unsaved walk in darkness, whereas believers should walk in light. What do you think he means by this contrast? (1 John 1:5-10)

3. List all the characteristics of the world mentioned in 1 John 2:15-17. Contrast this with the advantages of loving the Father (John 14:23; 15:8-11, etc.).

4. A study has shown that the TV viewing habits of Christians and non-Christians are about the same. Discuss the implications of this statement in light of Colossians 3:1-3.

5. In what ways might we subtly imply that Christ is not able to deliver us from the power of sin? In what ways can we correct this misapprehension?

2

The Consequences
of Sexual Sin

I begin with David. Not merely because his sin with Bathsheba is already well known. Nor because his story is given so many chapters in the Bible. Nor because his sin is unusual. I begin with David simply because *he's the last man we would expect to find in such a mess!*

After all, David was

• a hero who killed Goliath with a single stone
• a poet who gave us most of the Psalms
• a mystic who passionately sought God
• a king chosen by God and described by the Lord as "a man after My own heart."

Yet *that* David committed adultery, then ordered a man be killed to cover it up. Responding to his glands rather than reason, he brought shame and disgrace to himself, his family, and his kingdom.

You've heard the story: The king was taking a late afternoon nap on the flat roof of his palace. When he awoke, he walked around and "from the roof he saw a woman bathing; and the woman was very beautiful in appearance" (2 Sam. 11:2).

The longer David gazed at her the more his sexual desires were aroused. His blood ran hot as his eyes were riveted on her shapely body. He watched in the glow of the setting sun.

There's a world of meaning in the simple phrase "he saw." David's eyes focused on the beautiful naked body. Unfortunately, at that moment, that is *all* David saw. What David did not see is most revealing. He *did not* consider the consequences—the untimely demise of his four sons who would die because of what he was contemplating in his heart. He did not anticipate the guilt, the shame, the murder of a man, or the eventual loss of his kingdom. Those concerns were far from his mind at that instant. Tomorrow didn't matter. Maybe he'd even get by with it and nobody would know. Besides, if he didn't invite Bathsheba over for the evening, he'd always wonder what she was *really* like; he'd regret that he didn't take the tantalizing opportunity of enjoying her sexual prowess. He fantasized about conquering a woman he'd never met. What is more, he believed he could make her feel like a woman—fully satisfied.

Let's analyze what happened. There on the rooftop David made the decision to invite Bathsheba to his palace. If he was going to reject the temptation, he should have done it then. Perhaps David thought, *I can enjoy this woman vicariously for a time and choose later whether I invite her to my bedroom.* Perhaps yes, perhaps no.

The time to choose against sexual sin is the moment the passions arise. If we entertain lust, rejecting our passion becomes increasingly difficult. The correct response never becomes easier; every passing moment makes choosing sin more likely. For example, those who read pornography have already made a decision to commit mental adultery; consequently, the decision to commit the act of adultery has also been made. Only the *with whom* and the *when* remain undecided.

Yielding to Pleasure

When David took a long look at Bathsheba, he was cutting the anchor and setting out on a river whose speed and size was rapidly increasing. Returning to shore would become more difficult by the moment. David wasn't thinking about how and when he would return. He enjoyed the sensation of being swept along by the euphoria he felt in his body. He yielded to the pleasure of the moment. He forgot that dangerous rapids were ahead.

The next step was predictable. David *sent* messengers to invite her into the palace. I wonder what he said to his servants! Maybe he made an offhand remark about his desire to become better acquainted with his neighbors and wondered who lived two doors down from the palace; or perhaps after finding out that she was the wife of Uriah, one of his mighty men, he used the ruse of wanting to better understand the problems of wives whose husbands were at war. Whatever the excuse, it worked.

The third action was that he "took her . . . and lay with her" (2 Sam. 11:4). We don't know to what extent Bathsheba cooperated with David. Did she give in because of the prestige of being in bed with the king? Did she have genuine affection for David? Did she still love her husband, Uriah? We'll never know.

We also don't know whether David thought about the possibility of her becoming pregnant. Maybe she told him that this was her "safe" time of the month, or perhaps she thought she wasn't able to have children. Most likely they didn't think long on these matters—their passions had to be satisfied regardless of the consequences. Whatever the outcome, it could be handled later. Only the present had meaning.

What if Bathsheba had not become pregnant? Perhaps the affair would not have been discovered; Uriah would not have been killed, and David's kingdom would have remained intact.

But can we be sure? If we really understand sin, we know we can't escape the judgment of God—even if our actions are unknown to men. We'll discover that sin has enough hidden consequences of its own, apart from public shame. Besides, we can't be sure David's liaison would have remained a secret. What if Bathsheba, overcome with guilt, would have told her husband? Or perhaps she would have used her secret to bribe the king. Possibly the servants who were sent to get her already suspected what happened.

What we *do* know is that she became pregnant and told David the news.

The Cover-up

The king then had to face the fact that this casual affair wasn't as casual as he had imagined. A relationship that began between "two consenting adults" suddenly involved a third person: a baby was on the way. Uriah was also involved. David decided that he would have to get Uriah to think that the child was his. The king had been checkmated. He lost the first game but he was determined not to lose the tournament.

Enter *Plan A*. David asked that Uriah be brought to Jerusalem under the pretense that he was to inform the king about the state of the battle in Rabbah. Were they winning or losing? The king would ask him. Then he would send Uriah home, hoping that he would make love to his beautiful wife. David would see that a gift accompanied the warrior in the hope that it would foster a romantic spirit that would lead the couple into the bedroom.

But Uriah didn't play David's game. We don't know what suspicions he might have had. Did Uriah wonder, "Why all this attention and these special privileges?" He told David he would not go home because he'd feel guilty if he enjoyed his wife when his comrades were fighting under difficult conditions. He stoutly refused the king's offer.

By then David was desperate. He must get Uriah home to make sure that the sin would not become known. After all, this was best for the royal family and the entire kingdom.

And so *Plan B* emerged. The king asked Uriah to stay another day so that the two men could eat together. David made him drunk, hoping that in the evening Uriah would go home, but the loyal servant stayed with David's servants and did not visit Bathsheba.

If Uriah had gone home and made love to his wife, would David actually have been cleared? Bathsheba would have been forced into both living and telling a lie, of pretending that the baby belonged to her husband and lying about the "premature" birth. The child would be a constant reminder of the painful secret that had to be guarded with multiple deceptions.

And David would have to live with the guilt of knowing that he was the father of a child who may later discover his true identity. The king would have to carry this secret in his heart, knowing that his action had grave consequences in the life of the child. He would also have to live with the fear that Bathsheba might tell Uriah. What if her guilt was too great to bear? Then there was the king's relationship with his wives—what affect would their husband's sexual affair have on them?

But let's return to the story.

David moved to *Plan C.* It was his trump card. He decided to have Uriah killed in battle so that Bathsheba could become his wife. He gave Uriah a letter to take to Joab, his military commander. It read in part, "Put Uriah in the front line of the fiercest battle and withdraw from him, so that he may be struck down and die" (2 Sam. 11:15).

Why would a good man become a murderer? Why would a good man kill a friend so loyal that he could be trusted to take a letter to his commander without opening it? *Shame causes us to manipulate the consequences of sin.* From earliest times man has tried to bypass the judgment of God. The human mind is capable of rationalizing any action the heart craves. We will pay any price to make ourselves look good. David would have been better off if he had admitted his sin outright, despite the humiliation and embarrassment. Instead, he added to his sin and God's judgment increased proportionately.

Joab obeyed the king's orders and a messenger returned to tell David that Uriah had been killed. David simply replied, "Thus you shall say to Joab, 'Do not let this thing displease you, for the sword devours one as well as another.' " Matter-of-factly, David said, "Well that's life—you win some and you lose some!"

How is the cover-up working? Bathsheba knew, as did Joab, and most likely the servants. Others would at least suspect when the baby arrived. David knew, and as he later confessed, his sin was "ever before him."

Most importantly, God knew. Sin cannot be hidden from Him. He saw to it that David's cover-ups would eventually be uncovered.

Therein lies the irony of it all: As human beings we are often more concerned about what people know than with what God knows. Yet it is the divine Lawgiver who personally supervises the punishment of those who tamper with His authority. However meticulously we shield our sin from men, it is open to the eyes of God. Vividly, the author of Hebrews wrote, "And there is no creature hidden from His sight, but all things are open and laid bare to the eyes of Him with whom we have to do" (Heb. 4:13).

Some Conclusions

Even at this point in David's escapade, we can draw some conclusions:

Anyone can commit sexual sin—the committed Christian as well as the casual Christian. Ministers, doctors, missionaries—all are susceptible.

A seminary professor suggested to his students that they find a second vocation because a percentage of them would have to leave the ministry because of infidelity. Just recently, I heard of a minister who became involved with another man's wife. He was the last person I'd ever expect to be involved in such a relationship. As in so many perplexities of life, the last are often the first.

If David who at times loved God passionately could commit adultery, we should not be surprised at our propensity to sexual sin. Though it need not happen to anyone, it *can*. Many who self-righteously said, "I never would!" must now shamefully confess, "I did."

Whenever I hear someone refer to another's failings in judgmental tones, I wince. Apart from the grace of God we are all potential candidates for sexual misconduct.

Passions have awesome power. David, Samson, and Jezebel are examples of the allurement of sexual desires. Our passions can exert a subtle and dictatorial power over us. We may be able to control our actions, but our minds are sometimes overtaken by sexual enticements. Unless we change our thought patterns, our firmest resolutions often collapse under the weight of sexual desire. We concur with Augustine, "There's nothing so powerful in drawing the spirit of a man downward as the caresses of a woman." His own inner conflicts which he found to be unbearable were only resolved when he yielded himself fully to God.

Respectable husbands have abandoned their wives and children, pastors have resigned from effective ministries, and wives have left families they dearly loved all because of sexual enticement. As one said, "I hate what I'm doing, but I can't help myself. There's a part of me that wants to change, there's a part of me that doesn't. As it stands now, I think I've made the choice to go and do my own thing."

I believe temptations today are greater than in previous decades. Pornography and X-rated movies inflame the passions and erode moral resistance. An 11-year-old boy found a pornographic magazine in the drawer of a motel room. He became so sexually stimulated that he seduced his sister. For years he was hooked on pornography while continuing his incestuous relationship. Through God's power he has partially recovered from the experience, but his sister has not. Rebellion, bitterness, and depression have followed her into her own unsuccessful marriage.

David Morley wrote, "The sex drive is so intense that it can cut across all lines of judgment and intelligence. It can make a man cheat, steal, or kill, or make him throw away all his wealth or talent in order to pursue it" (*His,* November, 1971, p. 7).

We've got latent passions that can be aroused to a fever pitch. It's like throwing a match into a can of kerosene.

Despite the power of our passions, God holds us fully responsible for our actions. When God sent Nathan to David, Nathan gave his message in the form of a story: There were two men in a city, one rich and the other poor. The poor man had but one little ewe lamb, yet when a traveler came to the rich man, the host stole the poor man's only lamb and prepared it for the feast (2 Sam. 12:1–4).

David was angry when he heard this and replied, "As the Lord lives, surely the man who has done this deserves to die. And he must make restitution for the lamb fourfold, because he did this thing and had no compassion" (2 Sam. 12:5–6). Nathan's response jolted David. "You are the man!" (v. 7)

David had more compassion for a lamb then he did for Uriah—another indication of how our passions distort our values. David was the man in the story who had stolen his neighbor's lamb, and God would discipline him for what he did even though it all began in a moment of unrestrained passion.

Is God Fair?
Is it right that we be judged guilty for what we really didn't intend to do? What about the responsibility of the woman, Bathsheba? Why should a man who has faithfully served the Lord for

20 years be judged harshly for one lapse in a moment of passion?

Furthermore, some say, we don't blame a dog for acting like a dog. Why should we be held accountable for doing what comes so naturally? As sexual beings, why can't we act out our sexuality?

If man were an animal as contemporary behaviorists teach, then we must agree that he should *not* be blamed for his actions. B. F. Skinner, who believes man *is* an animal, teaches that there is no human responsibility—whatever people do, they just do. No blame should be attached to their actions.

The Bible presents a different view of man: He has a soul or mind as well as a body, and because a part of him is immaterial, he is not merely a cog in the machine, a victim of forces beyond his control. True, he is deeply fallen; he is born in sin, and does sinful acts. In fact, he cannot change his basic corrupt nature, but he *can choose* to restrain his actions regardless of the thoughts in his mind. In some Muslim countries where rape is punished by crucifixion and stealing by having one's right hand cut off, the crime rate is negligible—proof that man need not "do whatever comes naturally."

David, despite the indiscretions of Bathsheba, did not *have* to commit adultery. He could have stopped staring at her and he could have decided against inviting her to the palace. Because he chose to sin, he was responsible.

However paralyzed we believe our wills to be in moments of temptation, we still do have wills, and we are accountable for our actions. The belief that we *must act on our feelings* is one of the subtle lies of passions.

Because man is basically corrupt, he cannot change his inner nature. As indicated, he can refrain from certain actions, usually with great difficulty, and because of overriding considerations; but God is pleased only when he does more than that. He *can choose* to cast himself on God's mercy and ask for strength in facing moral choices. God is available to help in moments of need. Moral weaknesses should be incentives to drive people to the Cross. Christ died so that sin's grasp might be broken.

God has given us a high standard, yet with it has made it possible for us to be both forgiven and morally free. Augustine, when contemplating the question of how a man can be acceptable to a holy God, said, "O God, demand what You will, but supply what You demand." God is not playing games with us. He expects more from us than we are capable of doing on our own, but He stands ready to help us meet His requirements.

The mercy of God is reserved for those who stop trying to give excuses for their behavior. If we take responsibility even when temptation presses to "do it," we are in the place of humility where God can meet our deepest needs. He knows that we are created from dust. He is aware of our weaknesses and our propensity to sin, yet *He cannot let us off the hook*. He is a holy God.

When we stop blaming Him and take full responsibility for what we have done, He is free to come to our aid. No excuses, no passing of the buck, no blaming God.

What about God?

When we commit sexual sin, God is the loser. When we sin, our first thought is whether we'll be punished. Will someone find out? Will God discipline us? Will we be able to cope with our guilt? Yet God is the One whom we ought to think of first. Nathan reminded David of how good God had been to him. " 'It is I who annointed you king over Israel and it is I who delivered you from the hand of Saul. I also gave you your master's house and your master's wives into your care, and I gave you the house of Israel and Judah; and if that had been too little, I would have added to you many more things like these!' " (2 Sam. 12:7-8) David's sin was an act of ingratitude. His choice of Bathsheba implied that God had been negligent in meeting his needs. The Lord's provision was not acceptable, good, and perfect. Every sin we commit is an indictment against God's goodness.

This attitude goes back to the Garden of Eden. Adam and Eve could freely eat of every tree except one. And what did Satan do? He blinded them to their privileges, and said that if God were good and had their best interests in mind, He would let them eat of the one that was forbidden. The first sin was based on the premise that God was evil rather than good.

Think of how good God had been to David! And God had even greater plans for David. " 'If that had been too little, I would have added to you many more things like these!' " In one passionate act David callously forgot God's loving-kindness. Often sexual sin is committed against a background of multiplied privileges and blessings: good parents, an evangelical church, an understanding of the Scriptures—all these and more have been given by God, yet many have defied His Word.

Sexual looseness begins with ingratitude. The first step to moral ruin is listed in Romans 1. "For even though they knew God, they did not honor Him as God, or give thanks" (v. 21), and the rest is history. Sin and unthankfulness always go together.

Speaking of a couple who had premarital sex, Roy Hession comments, "And the greater loser in it all is God, the One whose heart was so different toward them from what they had thought, the One who was planning such good, greater than they had imagined, but whose purposes of love they have spoiled" (*Forgotten Factors,* Christian Literature Crusade, p. 60).

God also loses because His reputation is tarnished. Nathan continues, "However, because by this deed you have given occasion to the enemies of the Lord to blaspheme, the child also that is born to you shall surely die" (2 Sam. 12:14). The enemies of God would be able to say, "David is like the rest of us—he talks about knowing God, but look at what he's done!"

I'm impressed that God doesn't try to keep David's sin hidden so that the enemies of the Lord might not be able to gloat over David's shame. God could have chastened David privately. News of what happened could have been confined to God's people. But God let the word spread to the heathen.

When a Christian sins, God never tries to keep it hushed up. His reputation is ruined along with the believer's. We're the opposite. We do everything to hide our sin while God is trying to expose it.

We'll never be serious about parting with sexual sin until we know how much it grieves God. Nathan asked David, "Why have you despised the word of the Lord?" (v. 9) David probably didn't think of it that way, but God did.

Joseph would not have resisted the daily enticements of Potiphar's wife if he had thought only about what the sin could mean to other people. All that could have been rationalized in the heat of the moment. After all, didn't he deserve a bit of pleasure considering how he was mistreated by his brothers? Couldn't he easily keep this from Potiphar who was gone all day? With such reasoning he might have concluded that sexual pleasure was worth the risks involved.

What kept him from sin? It was his profound understanding *that God would be grieved.* "How then could I do this great evil, and sin against God?" (Gen. 39:9)

In sexual sin, both partners are hurt, but worse, God is hurt. They are saying to Him: "You haven't been good to me. I know more than You about what is best for me. I'm not concerned about Your reputation." Even when sin is skillfully hidden, God gets the same message. Imagine the grief of God!

Study and Application

1. Someone has said, "Idle hands are the devil's workshop." Discuss this statement in light of David's stay in Jerusalem (2 Sam. 11:1).

2. Study Psalm 32 and describe what David experienced during the time (perhaps a year) when he refused to repent of his sin.

3. In what ways are we vulnerable to sexual temptation and what can we do to minimize it?

4. Think of how our sin affects God. Can you cite instances where God expressed deep emotion because of man's sin?

5. Reread Nathan's words to David (2 Sam. 12:7–15). What thoughts did these words bring to David's mind? What is God's response to hidden sin?

3

Why Shouldn't I?

The barriers against premarital sex have all but crumbled. Adultery among consenting adults is chic.

Statistics tell the story: There are now about 300,000 teenage abortions per year, 250,000 illegitimate children, and an estimated 12 million young Americans with sexual diseases. Then there are all of the "consenting adults" who have extramarital affairs and who believe that sexual purity is no longer reasonable in our advanced society.

Everyone doesn't do it, of course. Those who don't are often ridiculed and accused of "puritanism." During the past two decades we've been told that the availability of contraceptives has made it possible to enjoy sex with a number of different partners without negative consequences. The playboy philosophy says you can hop from bed to bed without any ill effects. No hearts are broken; there's no rejection, no guilt, no sexually transmitted disease, or pregnancy. The more liaisons developed, the better chance for satisfaction and fulfillment. Millions have believed this illusion.

Young people particularly are fond of asking: "Why is sex

outside of marriage wrong? Is it really wrong, or is it wrong just because God said so?"

These are fair questions. Too often the impression is given that the Bible's teaching on morality has no rationale. We must follow its precepts blindly, quite apart from asking *why?* I believe that we ought to follow the teachings of the Bible, even if we don't understand the reasons for all of its commands. God knows more than we do, so we should submit to His authority even if we don't understand all of the reasons. He sees the whole picture; we don't. If time doesn't prove God correct, eternity will.

However, both from the Bible and from experience we can give powerful reasons for chastity. Young people who abstain from premarital sex are actually doing themselves a favor.

The High Cost of Guilt
Paul exhorted the people of Corinth to live in sexual purity, "Do you not know that the one who joins himself to a harlot is one body with her? For He says, 'The two will become one flesh'" (1 Cor. 6:16). Paul is talking about the oneness that transcends the physical—the kind of spiritual unity that properly belongs to the marriage relationship.

For those who believe in free love, sex is primarily a physical experience. When you're hungry you eat, when you're tired you sleep, and when you're turned on, you have sex. Such reasoning may sound right, but it's off the target by a mile.

We need some background to understand why. Thoughts are more than chemical reactions in the brain. The mind is a spiritual entity. As a pianist uses a piano to make music, so the mind uses the brain, which in turn affects other parts of the body through the nervous system. The brain is the part of the body where the spiritual and physical interact. The spirit can exist independently of the brain—it is eternal.

The point? God created us so that we cannot be sexually satisfied unless we are joined to our partner spiritually as well as physically. That's why so many people become emotionally damaged as a result of sex outside of marriage. The sex act can be pleasurable physically, but without the spiritual context, the partners will be hurt. There must be total commitment to one person. Because of the intimacy of the sexual experience, it cannot be satisfying apart from being assured that it will be repeated with the same partner.

Without a clear conscience there cannot be an uninhibited *giving,* a psychological blendings of the personalities. Something inside will always be unsatisfied and wrong. Recently, I read that 85 percent of our psychic energy goes into coping with guilt. God has made us in such a way that we cannot violate His Laws without experiencing the dead weight of psychological guilt.

Of course people will tell you that they don't feel guilty. A person who rationalizes his sin will always give the impression that he's not doing wrong. But suppressed guilt crops up as depression or anger. It breeds insensitivity and frustration. As one person put it, "Even though I rationalized what I was doing, I was dying by the inch inside."

In her book *Tough and Tender* (Fleming H. Revell, pp. 132–3), Joyce Landorf tells of a man who came to her husband to ask why life seemed to be so pointless. In part, he said:

> You know, Dick, I've really got it made. I'm free from the attachments of marriage. I've got this great pad at the beach and I go to bed with one sexy gal after another. I come and go as I please and I do my own thing. But something is really bothering me and I can't figure it out. Every morning as I get dressed for work, I look into the mirror and think, what was last night's sexy little game all about? Sure the girl was good looking. She was good in bed and she left this morning without bugging me, but is that all there is in life? I asked myself, *"If this lifestyle*

is what every guy thinks he wants, why am I so depressed? Why do
I feel a cold nothingness all the time?"... I know the guys here
think it would be fantastic to have this kind of liberated freedom
but honestly, Dick, I hate this life.

Here's an example of guilt smothering the satisfaction of
sexual relationships. The human spirit is torn apart because sex
is more than a physical relationship but a spiritual union as
well.

In Genesis we read, "Adam knew Eve his wife" (Gen. 4:1).
Use of the word *know* for sexual intercourse was not an attempt
to camouflage the sex act in obscure language. Sexual
intercourse is the highest kind of *knowing;* it's the clearest
expression of psychological and emotional unity.

By contrast, animals have no spiritual dimension. Consequently, for them sex is purely biological. They do what
comes naturally without any questions about trust or morality.
But we cannot break God's Laws without suffering the
psychological consequences. The damaging effects of guilt
cannot be avoided.

The Loss of Respect

Free love brings a man to the level of animals. It is following
desires wherever they happen to lead without responsibility.
Sex is reduced to biological pleasure. Jude refers to those who
are immoral as "unreasoning animals" (v. 10). Paul wrote that
God has given some over to "degrading passions" (Rom. 1:26).
It is the misuse of sex that makes us subhuman. Respect, which
is necessary for a fulfilling sexual relationship, is gone.

That's why a married man who slept with numerous women
concluded, "All that women are good for is sex. Apart from that
I wouldn't give you two bits for them." Notice that in separating
the biological from the spiritual (as one must do when living
promiscuously), he saw women as existing solely to satisfy his

passions. Their value as persons was irrelevant. He degraded women and he also degraded himself.

"But," replies the anxious young man to his pastor as he sits with his arm around his girlfriend, Jan, "I am one with Jan; we have unity and trust in our relationship. Why do we have to wait until we get a marriage certificate? What good is a piece of paper anyway? The point is we plan to be married."

Whether he realizes it or not, seeds are planted during premarital relationships that bear fruit years later. I've known many marriages to fall apart because of premarital sex. The wife reasons, "If he talked me into going to bed with him before marriage, what would prevent him from doing the same with another woman?" Or a man may become insanely jealous about his wife. He may be so filled with suspicions that he checks the speedometer of the car to see whether she has made an extra trip. Almost always such a couple has had premarital or extramarital sex. Jealousy and depression are often rooted in the soil of permissiveness. Guilt and mistrust erode self-respect.

Furthermore, a couple may intend to be married but the best rationalizations backfire.

Susan and Mike had been living together for several years and now they wanted to legalize their relationship. While she was making plans for the wedding, Mike met a former girlfriend at a party. Smoldering fires were quickly ignited. He and Doris fell in love again and within a week were in bed together. Mike called Sue on the phone to cancel the wedding or at least to postpone it until he had time to "get his head together."

Sue argued that Mike owed her marriage. After all, she had given herself to him for three years—that ought to be worth something! Mike disagreed. He admitted he had promised to marry her but didn't believe that such promises were equivalent to a vow. Furthermore, the fact that they had sex together didn't obligate him to marriage. Obviously, if sex were

equivalent to marriage many men would have to be poly-
gamists. He felt that he had no commitment to Susan and could
marry Doris.

Either way they couldn't win: To cancel the wedding meant
that Sue would feel cheated; to go ahead with it meant that
Mike would be conned into a marriage he didn't want. Imagine
the lack of excitement as such a couple approaches their
wedding day. Instead of anticipating sex, they are just going
through the routine of a marriage ceremony. It's like opening
your presents before Christmas.

I'm tired of hearing about sexual freedom. It's a lifestyle
fraught with broken promises and empty talk about love, and
replete with feelings of guilt, selfishness, and bitter betrayal.
Whatever physical pleasure is involved cannot compensate for
the spiritual and emotional damage that accompanies such
behavior.

As Warren Wiersbe says, "Young people are plugging their
6-volt toys into a 220-volt generator and blowing all their fuses
before they have a chance to live" (*Be Challenged*, Moody
Press, p. 2).

Permissiveness Leads to Other Sins

Since sexual permissiveness deadens the conscience, it should
not be surprising to learn that sexual sin leads to other kinds of
degrading behavior Recently, a man called me from a southern
state. He'd read my book *How to Say No to a Stubborn Habit*
(Victor). Tests, he told me, revealed that he was intensely
angry. On a scale of 1 to 100 he was a 96. A psychiatrist told
him that he was the angriest man he had ever seen. What would
cause such a man to be so frustrated and filled with rage? He
had a happy home life as a child, was successful as a mechanic,
and enjoyed a relatively satisfying marriage.

Soon the truth came out: He had had some recent homosexual experiences. The guilt brought him such frustration that he

wanted to lash out and commit suicide. Why? Because unresolved guilt leads to self-hatred, and self-hatred leads to hostility. This is why pornography and immorality of all kinds can lead to violence. When a criminal's apartment is searched, it almost always contains hard-core pornography and other perverse paraphernalia. I'm told that many X-rated movies portray violence as well as explicit sex. Sex on the screen is not a tender, caring relationship.

Police can usually tell if a murder was done by a sexual deviate because of the overkill. If the victim has numerous stab wounds instead of a half dozen, it shows that the murderer has outrageous hostility and anger.

This explains why rape is not so much a crime of sex as it is a crime of violence. Anyone who is unrestrained sexually will experience such self-hatred that he will no longer care about self-respect and decency. He has acted out his sexual fantasies so why should he not act out his desire to humiliate a woman? In a world where morality has become a matter of personal preference, what difference does it all make? To a polluted mind and conscience, anything is permissible (see Titus 1:15–16).

Wife beating is reaching epidemic proportions in the United States. Many women leave home frightened because of the unpredictable rage of a hostile husband. Child abuse is rampant with as many as 2 million children a year starved, beaten, or tortured. A recent report said that the statistics have more than doubled in the past few years. Occasionally children are even beaten to death by frustrated parents who are propelled by inner hostility.

Then there is sadomasochism and incest. One out of every 10 children may carry the dreaded secret of sexual relationships within the family. Almost always it is the result of a father who has relations with his daughter. In the past it was believed that the averge age of an abused daughter was 12 to 15, but now children between the ages of 5 and 10 are being sexually abused. It is impossible to calculate the inevitable fear, self-hatred, depression, and suicidal tendencies that will emerge in the life of such an abused child. In San Jose, California, 5 percent of the grade school children are in therapy because of sexual exploitation. No one can even estimate the number of cases that are unreported.

The connection between sexual immorality and a dead conscience that is capable of any act of cruelty is clearly taught in the Scriptures. Peter wrote, "And especially those who indulge the flesh and its corrupt desires and despise authority. Daring, self-willed, they do not tremble when they revile angelic majesties. But these, like unreasoning animals, born as creatures of instinct to be captured and killed, reviling where they have no knowledge, will in the destruction of those creatures also be destroyed" (2 Peter 2:10, 12).

Sin is never isolated. Tolerate it in one part of our lives and it will encroach on another. If we rebel against one of God's commandments it will be easier to violate others as well. No one has found a way to control sin's consequences.

God's Watchdog
Sexually transmitted disease is God's watchdog on promiscuity. The September 18, 1981 edition of the *Chicago Tribune* had a lengthy article about veneral disease—now referred to as sexually transmitted disease. According to this report, 1 of every 10 women, age 15 through 35, can expect to become unintentionally sterile by 1990 as a result of the nation's growing epidemic of sexually transmitted diseases. There are at least 1 million infections a year causing female infertility at the rate of 150,000-200,000 cases annually. "Nobody really likes to talk about sexually transmitted diseases," said Dr. James W. Curan, chief of the Operational Research Branch of the Atlanta Center's VD Control Division. "People, including those in the medical profession, do not realize how serious this problem is. If this

were some other disease, everyone would be alarmed and something would be done about it.

"These diseases pose serious health and social problems. Everyone should understand that there are serious medical complications to them, including sterility and hazards to the health of mothers and infants," he said.

The dangers of these diseases had previously been underestimated. Now they are blamed for sterility in women and men, life-threatening pregnancies, stillbirth, neonatal deaths, deafness, mental retardation, and other chronic disabling disorders. To summarize some of the consequences of more than 20 different kinds of sexually transmitted diseases, the article states that:

• More than 900 women die annually from various complications of pelvic inflammatory disease.

• The direct and indirect costs of that disease amount to $2.7 billion a year. More than 112,000 women are hospitalized with it each year.

• In 1980 there were 858,000 cases of pelvic inflammatory disease; 20 percent of the women became sterile.

• Life-threatening ectopic (outside the uterus) pregnancies skyrocketed, from 19,300 in 1971 to 41,000 in 1976. Most of these were caused by the disease which partially blocks the fallopian tubes so that a fertilized egg cannot migrate into the uterus.

• Chlamydia-infected mothers can pass the germ to their newborns during birth. Annually this causes 75,000 cases of conjunctivitis, an eye infection, and 30,000 cases of pneumonia.

• A leading cause of blindness in third world countries, Chlamydia also increases the risk of miscarriages and stillbirths.

• Between 300,000 and 400,000 teenage girls will develop pelvic inflammatory diseases this year causing infertility in one of five.

• Ten to fifteen million people have been infected with genital herpes, a lifelong disease that has periodic flare-ups and remissions. Genital warts affect 500,000 people each year and pubic crabs and lice are pandemic.

Researchers attempt to treat these diseases as a health matter, but it's also a matter of morality. It's one more way that society pays for its rebellion against God's established laws.

The Law of Diminishing Returns
Robert Burns wrote:

> But pleasures are like poppies spread:
> You seize the flow'r, its bloom is shed;
> Or like the snowfalls in the river,
> A moment white—then melts forever.

The irony of sexual misconduct is that there is no freedom to enjoy the satisfaction it promises. Satisfaction diminishes while desires increase. Arrive at one destination, there's always farther to go. To maintain the same erotic pleasure calls for experimenting with new thrills. That's why unbridled sex often leads to alcoholism and drugs.

The imagery of fire is used to describe unfulfilled lust. Paul spoke of those who were, "burned in their desire toward one another" (Rom. 1:27). Quite literally, unfulfilled burning lust is a taste of hell. And just as the fires of hell are never quenched, so is the person who is consumed by lust, "Sheol and Abaddon are never satisfied, nor are the eyes of man ever satisfied" (Prov. 27:20).

In his book *Sexual Suicide* (The New York Times Book Co., p. 42), George Gilder referred to the sexual revolution:

> Erotic activity became a shapeless, dissolute, and destructive pursuit of evermore elusive pleasures by evermore drastic techniques. In the quest for a better orgasm or more intense titillation, a frustrated population goes on ever wilder goose chases ... but always returning to the increasingly barren and shapeless lump of their own sexuality.

Hell itself is compulsive desires that are unsatisfied. Fires rage within the soul but are never quenched. The rich man didn't have a single drop of water to cool his tongue (Luke 16:24). Whatever the external torments of hell, the inner fires will be worse. Those who give themselves to unbridled sensuality already know the torture of being tied to passions they both love and hate.

Contrast True Love

In 1 Corinthians 7 Paul discusses the sexual relationship within marriage. He says, "Let the husband fulfill his duty to his wife, and likewise also the wife to her husband. The wife does not have authority over her own body, but the husband does; and likewise also the husband does not have authority over his own body, but the wife does" (vv. 3–4). Note that the good of the other is to be uppermost in each partner's mind. Real love is essentially unselfish.

Casual love and real love are in sharp conflict. Of course, there's nothing wrong with the natural sexual attractions among people. We meet someone whose appearance and personality are stimulating and we enjoy his or her company. So far so good. But if we marry on that basis, we're apt to meet someone else who is more attractive, winsome, and sexually stimulating. Such love is subject to change because its object may lose appeal. Some marriages make it on the strength of purely human love, but they are few.

The New Testament concept of love is a commitment to do what is best for the other person. Infatuation says, "I can't wait." Love says, "I will pay any price to treat you with respect. I'm willing to wait."

That's why the expression *free love* is a contradiction. If it is love, it is never free. It entails sacrifice on the part of the lover. If it's free, it's not love.

Sex, of course, is a part of married love but it is not

synonymous with love. One can exist without the other. Often couples have had sex without the slightest understanding of a loving commitment. On the other hand it is possible to have love without sex. In the case of illness or some physical deformity sex may be impossible, but love can endure such strains.

Because we're born selfish, our natural tendency is to want our passions satisfied quite apart from whether it helps or hurts our partner. "I love you," a boy tells his girlfriend but perhaps a more accurate statement would be, "I love myself; I *want* you."

What better way to prove love to someone than to forego sexual pleasure for the good of that one. After all, a man or woman's honor and good conscience are precious possessions. Why not agree to a standard and stick to it at any cost?

Who Owns Your Body?

Sexual temptation represents the clearest opportunity we have to declare our allegiance to Christ. Paul said, "Or do you not know that your body is a temple of the Holy Spirit who is in you, whom you have from God, and that you are not your own? For you have been bought with a price: therefore glorify God in your body" (1 Cor. 6:19–20). He argued for sexual purity on the premise of ownership. In the Old Testament the Shekinah glory stayed in the holy of holies; today the special dwelling place of God is within Christians. To be joined to another sexually apart from marriage is unthinkable. It's like taking an animal into the holy of holies. Paul says it is taking the members of Christ's body and joining them to a prostitute.

There's no easy answer to sexual temptation. Our passions sometimes urge us to sacrifice the permanent on the altar of the immediate. That's why we must give up our rights to our own bodies. We've got to acknowledge Christ's ownership of us—fully. Sinful pleasures are to be exchanged for other kinds of pleasures: "Thou wilt make known to me the path of life; in

Thy presence is fullness of joy; in Thy right hand there are pleasures forever" (Ps. 16:11, KJV). God has not restricted us to cheat us, but to give us a higher satisfaction.

Study and Application

1. Carefully study 1 Corinthians 6:12–20 by answering the following questions. A commentary might help.

a. Paul gives three reasons for sexual purity. Each is introduced with the question: Do you not know? State these in your own words.

b. Why do you think immorality is different from all other sins? (v. 18)

c. What indications are there that Paul considered sex to be a spiritual as well as a physical act?

d. What implications do verses 19–20 have for sexual purity?

2. Read Proverbs 7 and describe the end result of immorality.

3. Memorize 1 John 2:15–17. List contrasts between the values of the world and the value of God's will.

4. Study the first sin (Gen. 3). What was the nature of the deception? What are the parallels between that temptation and sexual temptation?

Yes, But . . .

"I don't feel any sense of wrong when we're together. . . . I thought I'd feel guilty but I don't. It's a fulfilling relationship for both of us."

He looked me squarely in the eye. He'd had a meaningless marriage for 10 years; now he's found someone who really understands him. She makes him feel like a man. Her alcoholic husband had neglected the family for years. He was the "great stone face," a man who simply could not communicate. There was no closeness, no warmth. Now this wife had found a man who could share his life with her. Didn't they (almost) have the right to an affair? What could be wrong with such a relationship?

Given the huge number of unhappy marriages, it's not surprising that partners meet others with whom they are better suited. The excitement of establishing a new relationship, the sense of self-worth that comes through being respected, and the exhilaration of a caring sexual relationship contribute to the feeling that it can't be all wrong.

Of course it can be beautiful. How else can we describe a relationship between a man and a woman who understand and complement each other? Such a relationship has even been credited with preserving the sanity of a partner. A woman with an unreasonable husband told me that apart from her affair with another man she'd "have gone crazy long ago." The joy of this new relationship was like finding an oasis in a desert.

Granted that the relationship is meaningful, and even caring, we still must ask: *At what price?*

An adulterer breaks at least five, and possibly six, of the Ten Commandments. The commandment "Thou shalt not commit adultery" (Ex. 20:14, KJV) settles the issue; but the question is still asked, "Is it wrong simply because God said it?" The answer is *yes*. If God is God, He has the right to determine its wrongness. In addition, adultery is intrinsically wrong because of the nature of man and woman. God is the Creator, and He set up the rules by which we are to function to achieve our greatest potential. When we break the rules of our Creator, it is sin.

God's Perspective

The word *adultery* not only refers to extramarital relationships but includes sexual looseness of all kinds. We have in this single commandment God's perspective on sexual misbehavior.

The commandment, "Thou shalt not bear false witness" (20:16, KJV) reminds us of another responsibility. The marriage ceremony is an oath made in the presence of God and other witnesses. In adultery, a vow is broken; the adulterer is backing out of a solemn promise.

Occasionally young people today say, "We're not going to have a marriage ceremony because it's so meaningless. A marriage certificate is just a piece of paper." I agree that the paper itself isn't what's important. Quite frankly, I couldn't find our marriage certificate if my life depended on it, but I *know* we've got one somewhere. In itself it is only a piece of paper filed away, but it's not that piece of paper that is important. It's what it signifies—I made an oath that obligates me to a lifelong commitment. It plays the same role as the contract I signed when I bought our house. No relationship exists where there is more to gain or lose than in the marriage relationship. No contract on earth has higher stakes. If one walks out of the agreement, the effects are devastating. Each partner needs to be absolutely sure that the other won't back out when the going gets rough. That's the purpose of a marriage ceremony: to make vows in the presence of witnesses so both partners can be held to their commitments. Adultery breaks these vows.

An adulterer bears false witness in other ways. He lies to his wife, making up excuses for coming home late. The Prophet Isaiah condemned the rebellious children who "add sin to sin" (Isa. 30:1). When we sin and try to cover it, we multiply our offenses. God said, "Thou shalt not bear false witness" (Ex. 20:16, KJV).

A third commandment reads, "Thou shalt not steal" (v. 15). As we saw in the story of David, adultery is stealing. To take someone's wife is to steal his most precious possession.

Perhaps now we are able to understand why a sexual relationship can be beautiful and caring, yet sinful and corrupt. The relationship may be satisfying, but the *method* in which it was attained breaks God's Laws. For example, suppose you were very hungry and you break into a store to steal food. You might say, "This is the best food I've ever tasted. How could steak that tastes so good be wrong for me to have?" The answer is that the food may taste good but you had to break one of the commandments to get it. "Thou shalt not steal" is still God's standard.

Coveting Is Rebellion

An adulterous relationship also breaks a fourth commandment, "Thou shalt not covet." Specifically, God says, "Thou shalt not covet thy neighbor's house; thou shalt not covet thy neighbor's wife nor his manservant or his maidservant, nor his ox, nor his donkey, nor anything that is thy neighbor's" (Ex. 20:17, KJV). To covet means to desire something that doesn't belong to us and thereby blame God because we've been shortchanged. *Coveting is rebellion against God.*

Also, God gave a commandment, "Honor thy father and thy mother" (Ex. 20:12, KJV). In almost every extramarital relationship people dishonor their heritage; they bring shame to their families.

Perhaps the most important commandment is the first, "Thou shalt have no other gods before Me" (Ex. 20:3, KJV). Whenever we elevate our passions above the will of God we have substituted our own god for the Lord God Jehovah. We are saying that we have *found a pleasure that is more precious to us than obeying our Creator.*

That's why the Christian man who sensed no wrong in his extramarital relationship was deceived. He thought that a caring relationship could justify his actions, but he didn't realize that he was shaking his fists at God in the process. Judas apparently loved silver. He betrayed Christ for 30 pieces, which he thought would satisfy his love of money. Was there anything wrong with having some extra silver? Of course not; I wish I had some myself! What made it wrong is that he denied Jesus Christ in order to get it. Adultery is evil because we have to shake our fists at God to have it.

Rationalizing

Consider some other rationalizations in defense of sexual misconduct:

We've all committed adultery in our minds, so the act doesn't make our sin more serious. "The way I look at it, we've all lusted in our hearts. Since lust is adultery anyway, what's the difference if I live with this divorcee?" That's the question a 35-year-old man asked after we learned that he'd been having an affair with an airline stewardess. Since she was no longer married, there seemed to be less reason to become concerned about this, the man thought.

Legally, there is no difference between an adulterous heart and an adulterous act because both are rebellion against God (Matt. 5:28). But there are other differences: Another person is involved as an accomplice to the rebellion. Though all sin is basically against God (as David learned), when we cooperate with others' sin we multiply our transgressions. The consequences of some sins are more serious than others. Lust can sometimes be forgiven without directly affecting one's relationship with others, but the sexual act cannot be easily forgotten because of the commitment involved. Because sex is a spiritual as well as a biological act, its misuse deeply tarnishes the soul. Paul wrote, "Flee immorality. Every other sin that a man commits is outside the body, but the immoral man sins against his own body" (1 Cor. 6:18).

Sexual sin is therefore different from all others because of the intimacy of the relationship with another human being. In fact, Paul wrote, "Or do you not know that the one who joins himself to a harlot is one body with her? For He says, 'the two will become one flesh" (1 Cor. 6:16). Over and above the union of two bodies is the union of two spirits which is recognized in the sight of God as a spiritual union. This does not mean that sexual intercourse is marriage. A man is not married to a prostitute because of his relationship with her; but there is a spiritual union that is recognized by God that defiles the body, mind, and soul. Those who engage in a sex act must bear greater consequences than those who sin only in the mind. It's simply not true to say that if we've done one we might as well do the other.

Don't I Deserve Happiness? "I have a right to happiness . . . this is probably my only chance. Furthermore, I should never have married Marvin in the first place. So why can't I have this relationship? I deserve it."

The Declaration of Independence states that we have "a right to life, liberty, and the pursuit of happiness," but this doesn't mean we are entitled to pursue happiness by any means such as rape or adultery. We have a right to pursue happiness only by lawful means. A right to happiness via adultery is purely selfish. Apparently, the partner being sinned against has no right to happiness, nor do the children.

I cannot pursue happiness unlawfully unless someone else relinquishes his or her right to happiness. Roy Hession wrote about adultery:

> Someone else paid the price of losing his life-companion; somebody else has shed tears far into the night; somebody else has been robbed of his happiness; somebody else has had his home broken up; somebody else has been left lonely, struggling along on his own; children have been left without a father or a mother. It is easy to forget the terrible wrongs another has suffered as we enjoy our new love (*Forgotten Factors*, Christian Literature Crusade, p. 22).

C. S. Lewis has observed that the principle of pursuing happiness by immoral means "once allowed in that department, must sooner or later seep through our whole lives. We thus advance toward a state of society in which not only each man but every impulse in each man claims *carte blanche*" (*God in the Dock*, Eerdmans, p. 322).

Can someone be happy while grieving the Spirit of God? What if Christ had bypassed the torture of the cross in the pursuit of His own happiness? Pascal commented wisely, "Happiness is neither out of us nor in us. It is in God."

We have an obligation to obey God and worship Him, but we are not obligated to be happy. "A right to happiness doesn't, for me, make much more sense than a right to be six-feet-tall, or to have a millionaire for your father, or to get good weather whenever you want to have a picnic" (Lewis, *God in the Dock*, p. 318).

No one has a right to pursue happiness at the expense of character. We have even less right to do it in defiance of God.

What about the argument, "I should never have married Marvin in the first place"?

Have we forgotten that God is a specialist at working in, through, and in spite of our mistakes and failures? No one blew it as badly as Adam and Eve. They had a perfect opportunity to obey, but their unbelief brought devastation to the whole human race. God did not let them evade responsibility; He promised to meet their need right where they were.

God's solution to one sin (a foolish marriage) is never for us to commit a second sin (to find some reason to break our marriage vow). He's more concerned about changing us than our circumstances. Patience within marriage is more honorable than seeking an exit from it. When we repent of sin, God uses those experiences to build maturity in us.

Some rationalize that *it's possible to sin moderately and be satisfied.* "I'd never go to bed with a woman but I do read pornography." A person thinks he is able to draw a line beyond which he will not go—he believes he is quite safe in his private world. I'm also thinking of the person who attends X-rated movies occasionally or reads sensual novels. He's the kind of person who sins vicariously. He would not commit adultery, but he watches soap operas and identifies with those who commit adultery. He may envy the path of the wicked, but so far he has stayed within the folds of the church—except of course in his private life and mind.

Let's remind ourselves that the more we feed our lower natures the stronger they will become. Consider an alcoholic who believes he can stop drinking at any time—and often he can, but his appetite for alcohol is growing steadily and soon he will not be able to say *no* regardless of how badly he wishes to do so.

So it is with sensuality: It may begin with pornography or an

X-rated movie, but soon it will lead to sexual acts. It's like feeding a small but hungry tiger. He's manageable now, but he will become a ferocious beast.

One young person said, "I thought if I went to see one X-rated movie I'd get all of the curiosity out of my system, but now I'm hooked."

Christ flatly denied that it's possible to sin and yet be in control of the situation. To commit sin is to be the slave of it (see John 8:34).

I've heard of people drifting in a boat on the salty ocean who became so thirsty that they insisted on drinking ocean water even though they had been warned not to do so. The water looked great and they were convinced it would slake their thirst. What they didn't realize was that a half cup of salt water would increase their thirst several times over. They would die of thirst sooner than those who restrained themselves and waited to be rescued. There is no such thing as taking a little bit of salt water and being satisfied.

Many years ago when he was Prime Minister of England, Cromwell attended a circus. An animal trainer came onto the imitation grass, cracked his whip, and a huge snake wrapped itself around his body. As the crowd hushed they could hear bones cracking and the animal trainer soon was dead. He had trained the snake for 13 years, after getting it when it was only 7 inches long. Back then he could have crushed it between his forefinger and his thumb. Because he thought he had it under his control he believed he was safe. He was quite wrong.

God's Word assures us that we can never keep sin contained. If we willfully yield to it, it will inevitably demand more until at last it's got all of us.

Whatever we rationalize, we must ask God to show us why it's a lie. For the flesh and the devil, deception is the name of the game. We should actually fear sin, knowing that we might become ensnared when we play with it.

You've heard it said that "the fear of the Lord" refers to the fact that we ought to reverence God, that we don't have to be afraid of Him. I was surprised to find that can't be proved biblically! Read passages such as Deuteronomy 6:13–15, where the fear of the Lord is directly linked to His anger and punishment.

How does God discipline us? By letting sin have more control over us. He gives us what we crave and more besides. The greater the rebellion, the greater the slavery.

We may say that nobody understands our situations. Maybe they don't, but God does. Though He loves us deeply, He never changes His mind because we're in a tough spot. He wants us to give up our rationalizations, regardless of the cost.

Study and Application

1. Proverbs 6:26–35 describes the sin of adultery. What other sins accompany adultery? What are the consequences listed?

2. Read Deuteronomy 6:4–9. Why do you think Satan would be so concerned about destroying homes? Why is adultery such an attractive means to this end?

3. Study Hebrews 13:4. What does the verse teach about marriage?

4. Read Revelation 18:2–8. By what standard does God judge the harlot Babylon? Does this teach us anything about the sufferings of eternal hell?

5

I'll Take My Chances

"I know chastity is right, but is it smart?" the young man wanted to know. "God may say that immorality is wrong, but even so, maybe a man is cheating himself out of euphoric pleasure for no really important reason," he continued. "Tell me the worst that could happen if I go ahead with it." He was weighing the pros and cons. His reasoning was straight forward: As long as the price wasn't too high, he would disregard God's opinion. Sure, he might have to pay for his sin, but if he could control the consequences he might get by rather cheaply. There are bargains everywhere—maybe he could find one for his sexual relationship. The forbidden pleasure may well be worth the price. He thought he'd take his chances.

Is disobedience ever worth the price? Must we always pay for sin or can we simply ignore the consequences and do our own thing? If the pleasure of sin would, even in one instance, compensate for the consequences, God would be rewarding sin!

We've all become accustomed to credit cards, which make it possible to enjoy almost anything now and pay later. The problem is that we do have to pay, and sometimes at exorbitant interest. We can't have the enjoyment without the slavery. Some sins have greater consequences than others, and the Apostle Paul singles out sexual sin (1 Cor. 6:18).

Sin is deceptive for three reasons. *First, it does pay some immediate dividends.* Let's be honest and admit that there is pleasure in sin. If sin was not enjoyable, the road of sensuality would not be so well-traveled. This means a lot to the *now* generation where the immediacy is all that counts.

Sin also deceives us because most of its consequences are hidden. James wrote, "But every man is tempted, when he is drawn away of his own lust, and enticed" (James 1:14, KJV). The expression "drawn away" has the idea of baiting a trap. A hunter leaves a chunk of fresh meat on the trap which is concealed in the snow. There are some immediate rewards for the bear who comes strolling by because the meat tastes good. All the ugly consequences are hidden from view.

The word *enticed* is used of baiting a hook. Again, there is both immediate gratification and concealment. The fish is promised something appealing without understanding the consequences. Since animals and fish are ignorant of how traps and hooks work, they are caught. They have no idea that suffering and death await them.

Similarly, it is easy to fantasize about the most exotic sexual experience and even be able to enjoy it temporarily as long as we are blinded to what's happening to ourselves and to others, and particularly to God who is grieved because of our disobedience.

Sin is deceptive because it appears controllable. Whenever we get by, we develop confidence in our own ability to control our passions. An unmarried couple may think that they are able to stop before sexual intercourse, and maybe they can. But every time they overstep God's boundaries their consciences are deadened and their defenses weakened. Even if they pride themselves in their technical chastity, they're bound to find other sins in their lives that are out of control. A double-minded man is unstable in all his ways (James 1:8).

One man, determined to brave heaven and hell to get what he wanted, said, "But you've got to admit that David did get his Bathsheba despite his sin!" True. So did Samson get his Delilah and Judas his silver. But think of how much they paid!

In Galations 6:7 we read, "Do not be deceived, God is not mocked; for whatever a man sows, this he will also reap." Paul warns us against deception; that is, thinking we can find some loophole in God's way of dealing with the world. It is foolish to think we can actually put one over on God!

We Reap What We Sow

Let's consider three laws of sowing and reaping. Sin always reproduces sin. Sometimes it is more of the same sin. David didn't consult the Lord about his marriages and ended up with seven wives. His immoral life led to greater immorality—he stole another man's wife and committed adultery. He lost in a moment what it took a lifetime to gain.

Sometimes we reap additional sins. The works of the flesh come in clusters; they tend to spawn other forms of disobedience. David began with adultery and ended with murder.

The principle applies to other sins as well. Dishonesty begets more dishonesty. Getting by with stealing once, leads one to try it again. Each time the grip becomes stronger.

How does God discipline His children when they sin? Usually we expect Him to send a bolt of lightning. Or perhaps we think that He permits accidents, or terminal illness. I think that God often *gives us more of what we want*. One immoral act leads to another, which in turn leads to another, but along with the enjoyment comes greater slavery.

Remember when the Children of Israel cried to God for meat? They hated the menu in the desert. Like gluttons today, they were insisting that they have more selection in their food.

God became upset with their sensual desires and said, "You shall eat, not 1 day, nor 2 days, nor 5 days, nor 10 days, nor 20 days, but a whole month, until it comes out of your nostrils and becomes loathsome to you; because you have rejected the Lord who is among you and have wept before Him, saying, 'Why did we ever leave Egypt?' " (Num. 11:19-20)

The discipline for wanting meat was lots of it! No doubt they enjoyed the meat for awhile, but soon it became disgusting. One who is enticed by the thrills of sensuality later discovers that he is bound by what he has now come to hate.

One sure sign of complete repentence is when we are afraid to fall back into our old sins, lest God judge us with even greater slavery. A person who had gained victory over his alcoholism told me that he would never take so much as one drink again. He's afraid that the cycle of bondage will start all over again. He has finally understood a basic principle. Whatever we sow we reap.

We Reap in a Different Season
Have you ever noticed how casual people are about sin? One of the reasons we have so many divorces among Christians is because we can all point to those who have left their partners for other women and who are now well-adjusted and happy. It seems as if God isn't as strict as He used to be. Maybe some of the consequences aren't happening anymore.

"Because God does not punish sinners instantly, people feel it is safe to do wrong" (Ecc. 8:11, TLB). I don't know why God is so patient with disobedience. He doesn't settle His accounts at the end of the month. He's willing to wait for the wild oats to ripen. If we entertain any doubts about God, we should remember that He never changes. He hates sin as much as ever.

We can liken a sinful lifestyle to a smorgasbord—taking whatever we want and paying later. Of course, the bills come due; character is eroded. The heart condemns (1 John 3:21), joy and assurance of God's guidance evaporate, relationships rupture. All this for the pleasure of sin. And that's not the end. The remote consequences are a wasted life, with no works that will survive the fire of God's judgment. Even for believers, the results of disobedience are priced right out of sight.

Think of all the children who are confused, hurt, and rejected because of an unfaithful mother or an alcoholic father. Consider the wasted life, the misguided values, the suspicion and hatred that sin brings in its wake. We have only a sliver of time on earth in comparison to endless eternity, yet God will judge us for how we spend these brief years and their impact for good or for ill will go on for eternity.

I'm convinced that many people will have to wait until they are in eternity before they believe that God was right, that sin is as bad as God said it is. The consequences are built right into the nature of sin and they cannot be bypassed. An unmarried couple might want to minimize some of the consequences. Birth control may cover their sin from the public eye, but God knows. God has promised, "He who conceals his transgressions will not prosper, but he who confesses and forsakes them will find compassion" (Prov. 28:13).

God's patience is not an indication that the sinner is getting by with his wrong.

We Reap More Than We Sow

We see this from the life of David. He thought he could keep his sin a secret, but God had other thoughts about David's immoral ways. God told David, "Indeed you did it secretly, but I will do this thing before all Israel, and under the sun" (2 Sam. 12:12). Later David's son Absalom committed immorality publicly. David thought he could keep it secret, but God said He would personally see to it that all would become public.

David had said that the man who stole the sheep should pay

fourfold. He didn't know he was speaking about himself. Four of his sons died prematurely. First, Bathsheba's son died. Second, Amnon raped his sister Tamar. Then Amnon was killed by Absalom because of this crime. Absalom in turn was killed later because he wanted to take the throne from David. And finally Adonijah was executed because he wanted to become king. In the end, David came back into fellowship with God, but his children didn't.

Sin is like yeast—a little bit leavens the whole lump. Its influence is much greater than its size or shape, and its consequences are unpredictable. No wonder we need a Redeemer to get us out of the mess! To try to do it ourselves is like attempting to mop the floor with the faucet running. God wants us to understand that sin is a high-priced item. Charles G. Finney wrote, "Sin is the most expensive thing in the universe. Nothing else can cost so much. Pardoned or unpardoned, its cost is infinitely great. Pardoned, the cost falls chiefly on the great atoning substitute; unpardoned, it must fall on the head of the guilty sinner" (*Great Sermons from Master Preachers of All Ages*, Zondervan, p. 93).

Again, Finney has written, "How many tears, poured out like water, it has cost; how much pain in many forms this enterprise has caused and cost; yea, that very sin which you roll as a sweet morsel under your tongue! God may well hate it when He sees how much it costs and say 'Oh do not that abominable thing that I hate!'" (*Great Sermons*, p. 107)

The idea that we can sin and take our chances began in the Garden of Eden. Eve thought she could satisfy her sensual appetite and actually enhance her own status. Was it really a reasonable gamble? The devastation that sin brought could never have been predicted. Throughout all eternity multitudes will be in torment because Adam and Eve disobeyed God.

Let's review what I call the cycle of disobedience.

First, we are in control. We set the limits of disobedience.

Second, we win some battles, are able to restrain ourselves, and have the feeling of being in complete command of the situation. We may believe we can stop whenever we want along the continuum of disobedience, but if we should miss some forbidden pleasures, we stay in the vicinity of the temptation.

Third, we weigh the pros and cons and conclude that we've made a wise choice. The fulfillment of our selfish desires outweighs any consequences we can forsee.

Fourth, we sign the contract. We commit ourselves to certain lifestyles, believing that there are exceptions—just for us.

Fifth, the terms of the agreement are suddenly changed. Just like Gehazi who thought he was getting gold, but ended up with leprosy (2 Kings 5:22–27); we realize that we didn't read the fine print.

Suddenly we're not in control and when we try to get out of our dilemma, we find our agreement is binding.

Sixth, Satan comes to collect. We can't believe what's happening. It is out of our hands.

Seventh, we are absolutely desperate and we ask God for a quick deliverance.

But God won't bail us out until we've learned our lesson. Those who work with alcoholics say there's no use trying to help them until they "bottom out." They've got to come to the end of themselves *totally.* By experience, they must be convinced of the high cost of drink.

Have you ever heard one caught in sin's grip say, "If I had only known." What they're actually saying is, "If I had only believed God." Every deliberate sin, is a choice against the guidance and goodness of God.

If we say, "I've learned to live with my guilt," we're actually saying, "I have learned to live in defiance of God."

Study and Application

1. What is the thrust of 1 Timothy 5:6?

2. Read Titus 1:15. What are the effects of a polluted mind and conscience?

3. Discuss the idea that we can sin deliberately and still be in control in light of John 8:34.

4. Contrast the way the world looks at the pleasures of sin with Paul's evaluation (Titus 3:3).

5. Apply to the United States (or any country) the three laws of sowing and reaping in this chapter.

6

I Can't Let Her Go

"Sure it's sin. I've tried—God knows I have—but I can't let her go."

His final words caught my attention. They came at the end of a long discussion with a man about his wife's failures and a concealed affair with a woman he truly loved. He said the words slowly and deliberately. "I can't let her go."

Being unable to let go also applies to other sins such as drug and alcohol addiction and gluttony, but breaking a relationship with another human being is more difficult. There has been a sharing of intimacies. For those in meaningless marriages the letting go of an affair is unthinkable. Those who were formerly married experience the same anguish at the thought of breaking off an affair. Abstinence seems unrealistic to one who has known the joy of sexual fulfillment. Death and divorce create a vacuum for a partner that can be fulfilled only through sexual closeness (or so it is claimed). To suggest otherwise brings the objection, "You don't understand!"

Yet God asks that the cherished desires of the heart be laid to rest. He knows that we are not at the mercy of our feelings, regardless of how loudly our passions protest. In the Scriptures we read, "No temptation has overtaken you but such as is common to man; and God is faithful, who will not allow you to be tempted beyond what you are able, but with the temptation will provide the way of escape also, that you may be able to endure it" (1 Cor. 10:13).

Consider Christ's startling statement: "But I say to you, that everyone who looks on a woman to lust for her has committed adultery with her already in his heart" (Matt. 5:28). With such a high standard all men are indicted! Lust is lodged in every human heart. How can such desires be brought under control? Christ anticipated our response. He knows that parting with lust is like getting rid of a part of our bodies.

So He continued: "And if your right eye makes you stumble, tear it out, and throw it from you; for it is better for you that one of the parts of your body perish than for your whole body to be thrown into hell. And if your right hand makes you stumble, cut it off, and throw it from you; for it is better for you that one of the parts of your body perish, than for your whole body to go into hell" (Matt. 5:29–30). The term *stumbling block* according to Barclay, means "bait stick in a trap." The picture is that of a pit dug in the ground and deceptively covered with a thin layer of branches carefully arranged so that the unwary traveler would step on it and fall into the pit. Christ is saying that if your eye or hand causes you to be tripped up—if you find yourself tempted sexually—take drastic action.

It is often through the eye—a look—that lust begins. Then perhaps tender words intensify the desire, and gentle caresses open up the floodgates of passion. Christ said that if it is necessary to cut off a hand or to pluck out an eye to keep sexually pure—do it! Unfortunately, His words are often dismissed because it is argued that He was speaking figuratively or that getting rid of one eye or hand is no safeguard; there's another of each.

Though Christ was not telling us to amputate parts of our bodies, He expects us to take action, to cut off the source of our lust or to remove ourselves from the temptation. He recognized striking parallels between parting with members of our bodies and saying *no* to our passions. He understood that both require extraordinary measures. Notice these parallels.

Amputation Is Painful

Sitting here in my study, I'm trying to visualize my right arm amputated; even worse, having my right eye removed. The thought is abhorrent. In ancient times there was no anesthetic, no way to alleviate the throbbing torment that would accompany surgery. No needles, helpful drugs, or delicate surgical instruments—just crude cutting tools. Grotesque scars remained as reminders of the ordeal. In our day anesthetics deaden the pain. It may be excruciating, but there is hope for recovery. Wounds heal and strength returns.

Christ knew that our hands and eyes are highly prized; we'd do anything to spare them. We wouldn't part with them unless it was absolutely necessary. Lust is as difficult to part with as a hand or an eye. Anyone who has experienced the exhilaration of sexual attraction knows that. Consider the man who is dreaming about his wrongful lover. Happiness (it appears) is within his grasp; yet he must say no when the prize is within his reach.

Recently I spoke to a man who was in love with another woman, but they decided to break off their relationship so that he could go back to his wife and family and rebuild a deteriorating marriage. He still had deep affection for the woman, and wondered why his emotions didn't change toward his wife. A healing process must take place, just as when a marriage partner dies. There will be grief, tears, and loneliness. Who can understand such emotional pain, yet Christ says, "Do it."

How?

First by getting away from the temptation. Paul's advice is,

"Flee immorality" (1 Cor. 6:18). And again, "Flee from youthful lusts" (2 Tim. 2:22). Run from temptation without leaving a forwarding address.

What if temptation is close—next door or at the job? The seed of sensuality must be crushed before it gets an opportunity to become firmly rooted in mind and body. Whatever it takes, stop it—it is sin sweetly poisoned.

Theaters, bars, and similar places appeal to fleshly desires. It may be necessary to change jobs to lessen the bombardment of sexual stimuli. Break relationships that have become doorways to allurement. Eliminate visits to newsstands that carry pornography and provocative paperbacks, and part company with friends who influence you to do evil (Prov. 1:10–19).

"There's no way I can escape temptation," you say. "It's where I work, and even changing jobs wouldn't guarantee immunity from further enticement."

True, but that doesn't negate Christ's words. Often we know precisely what we could do to counteract the inroads into our private world of passion.

We must ask God to "lead us not into temptation." Daily we are confronted with sin in a hundred different disguises. God can direct us to avoid the pitfalls; He can keep us from stumbling. If we ask Him, He will shield us from circumstances that are particularly vulnerable. "The Lord knows how to rescue the godly from temptation, and to keep the unrighteous under punishment for the day of judgment" (2 Peter 2:9).

When we flee, we have God on our side.

We must fling the stumbling block aside, treat it as a woman would a mugger. It is not the time for sweet negotiations and a drawn out farewell. We should never treat sin with compassion and compromise.

Saying no to our passions is painful but possible. Many have had an eye removed or an arm amputated when gangrene has set in. They endured the suffering to contain the poison. Christ knew it wouldn't be easy. Yet He asked us to do it for our own good and for His name's sake.

Amputation Is Thorough

Suppose you go to a doctor with a cancerous growth on your arm and he says, "I plan to do this in stages; I'll cut out most of it this time and take more later. We won't decide now whether we eventually will take it all."

Absurd? Of course. You want him to cut a trifle beyond the growth to make sure he's got it all. You want the surgery to be final. Once the decision has been made, you can't rethink it.

This should also be true of sexual sin. Benjamin Needler, a Puritan writer, put it this way: "We must not part with sin, as with a friend, with a purpose to see it again and to have the same familiarity with it as before, or possibly greater. . . . We must shake our hands of it as Paul did shake the viper off his hand into the fire" (*Puritan Sermons,* Richard Owen Roberts Publishers, p. 53).

How can this be applied? We are to burn every bridge behind us—no turning back (remember Lot's wife). Just as the ancient Jews searched their houses with a candle to be sure that there was no leaven left among them, we must with the same diligence search our lives lest there be a bit of poison that deadens our whole body. Pull it out, though it resists like a tooth in the jaw.

What opens the door to sexual vulnerability? Television? Movies? Delighting in another's wife or husband. In Romans we read, "Put on the Lord Jesus Christ, and make no provision for the flesh in regard to its lusts" (13:14).

When I speak of making a complete break with sin, I don't mean just sexual sin. *Any sin we tolerate can be the cause of failure in sexual temptations.* Paul taught that immorality, impurity, sensuality, idolatry, sorcery, and other sensual sins have a common root—the flesh (see Gal. 5:19–21). Compromise in one matter leads to problems in another. Unresolved anger can lead to drunkenness; dishonesty to immorality.

Any counselor knows that cause-effect relationships in behavior are skillfully hidden. Why are we overcome by the same sin again and again? Often it's because we haven't probed deeply enough; we may be denying God access to all areas of life. This is illustrated by a remarkable story in Joshua 7. Israel was routed when fighting the men of Ai. Joshua and his army lost 36 men in the skirmish. If a military expert were to analyze the cause of the debacle, what would he say? He'd evaluate the army, study its tactics, and recommend sophisticated equipment along with a better strategy. He'd give a timetable for beefing up the Israelite war machine so that the enemy would be subdued quickly and with a minimum of casualties.

Actually the strength of Israel's army had little to do with its defeat or victory. The real cause was that Achan had stolen a garment which was to have been destroyed along with the city of Jericho! No secular man could make such an analysis. On the surface there was no connection between a stolen garment and a defeated army, but God established such connections.

Because of the common root of sin (rebellion) one sin, however distantly related, can be the cause of another. The forces that open the heart's door to lust may be fed from a different source.

A man who could not overcome the habit of buying pornography found that this sin's power was broken when he thoroughly repented of other sins which he had conveniently overlooked. These included returning stolen items, asking his parents to forgive his rebellion, and confessing his anger at God for his predicament in life.

You might not think that cheating on your income tax can lead to failing in sexual temptation, but it can. If covetousness caused a military defeat, it can cause a moral defeat as well.

That's why rock music can lead to sensuality and guilt to anger—ultimately, all sin is related and it has random consequences. A. W. Tozer wrote, "That part of ourselves that we rescue from the Cross may be a very little part of us, but it is likely to be the seat of our spiritual troubles and our defeats."

Take an unhurried half hour and pray with the psalmist, "Search me, O God, and know my heart; try me and know my anxious thoughts; and see if there be any hurtful way in me, and lead me in the everlasting way" (Ps. 139:23–24).

Amputation Is Worthwhile

Is the pain worth it? Ask the cancer patient who has been told by his doctor, "We got it all!" The exhilaration of a physical cure fades in comparison with the advantages of moral freedom. Christ said that if in a choice between losing an eye or losing the soul, it would be foolish to opt for an eye. The soul is worth more. To ruin the soul through guilt and shame (even if we'll be saved as by fire) is a high price to pay for forbidden pleasure. Christian Bovee said, "The body of a sensualist is the coffin of a dead soul."

The handicapped man with only one hand and one eye is unable to fulfill his cherished dreams. The hopes of a lifetime are shattered. He really has no option except to adjust to a host of unfulfilled desires. He'll have to bury his plans and redirect his life toward simpler goals. He'll either readjust or self-destruct.

Christ knows our disappointments. Yet He says, "It is better to live without companionship than to have it in defiance of God. It's preferable to go through life with a tumultuous marriage and be able to claim God's friendship than to be fulfilled and incur God's disfavor. God is a friend of the lonely, frustrated, and tempted; but He will judge those who commit immorality. "For fornicators and adulterers God will judge" (Heb. 13:4).

Walter Trobisch spoke with insight, "The task we have to

face is the same, whether we are married or single: to live a fulfilled life in spite of many unfulfilled desires" (*Love Is a Feeling to Be Learned,* InterVarsity Press, p. 18).

Sexual sin, however appealing, is never worth more than an arm or a leg. Someone has said, "How prompt we are to satisfy the hunger and thirst of our bodies; how slow to satisfy the hunger and thirst of our souls." And somewhere I read this bit of advice: When we have to jump over a chasm, it's better to do it in one long jump rather than in two short ones! We need to obey instantly—whatever the cost.

Breaking the Relationship

Let's return to the man who said, "I can't let her go." The two appear to be perfectly suited but God has said *no.*

A feeling of indebtedness has developed. They've voluntarily given themselves to the most intimate of all relationships, and the woman may say to him, "If you leave me I'll commit suicide—you're the only person in the world who understands me." Or she may say, "If you leave me I'll spread it all over town. I'll slander you—you've got more to lose than I."

What can the man do?

He can approach her in a spirit of humility. Confess his part of the sin. It's useless to argue who is responsible; to a lesser or greater degree both are. He should help her to see that he is genuinely sorry that he robbed her of intimacy—that he stole what he did not own; and took a path that leads to destruction. He can tell her that this is the end. It's final.

He should be willing to submit to any discipline the Lord might allow. Fear of exposure must not prevent confessing and forsaking sin. The detour is always rougher than the main road.

Whatever happens, it will likely be less serious than losing an eye or a hand. No one has succeeded in making the way of the trangressor easy.

Yes, you can let her go.

Study and Application

1. In light of 2 John 6, what does a person's willingness to put away sin say about his love for God?

2. Does God ever ask believers to do the impossible? If not, how do we receive the enablement to do what we should?

3. Since the eyes are usually involved in sexual temptation (Matt. 5:28), what practical steps are necessary to keep ourselves pure? How can Christians help one another in this?

4. If a man falls in love with another man's wife, what steps can be taken to *rebuild* the existing marriages?

5. In Genesis 22 we have an example of a man who was willing to set aside all human affection to do the will of God. What blessings did he receive as a result of obedience?

7

Is It OK if I Do
It by Myself?

Possibly one of the most widespread sexual practices among young people is masturbation. "No other form of sexual activity has been so frequently discussed, so roundly condemned, and more universally practiced, than masturbation" ("Autoeroticism" in *The Encyclopedia of Sexual Behavior,* edited by A. Ellis and Aborbanel, Vol. I, Hawthorne Books, p. 204). The guilt associated with this practice is often excessive. Just last week I received a letter that read, "Please help me . . . I masturbate. Is there any hope? I've even thought of suicide."

A generation ago masturbation was almost unanimously condemned by Christian counselors and pastors. But times have changed. Today some Christian youth leaders tell young people that it isn't a sin unless done too frequently. James Dobson in his film series, "Focus on the Family," says that unless it is done excessively or as a substitute for intimacy in marriage, it should be accepted as a normal part of growing up.

Several arguments favor this approach. Almost every young man and a good percentage of young women have at some time practiced masturbation. Whatever struggles a person may have with it, he or she can at least be consoled that they have plenty of company.

Also, this practice has no harmful physical effects. Contrary to the dire warnings of past generations, it does not produce insanity or make one more susceptible to disease. Such fears, which were intended to discourage the practice, were ill founded.

However, perhaps the most oft repeated argument in favor of a more relaxed attitude is that masturbation usually is accompanied by excessive and destructive guilt. The logic is obvious: if it is accepted as a legitimate sexual outlet, the guilt will vanish.

Though the Bible condemns all kinds of sexual sin, it makes no explicit reference to masturbation. The expression, "abusers of themselves and with mankind" (1 Cor. 6:9, KJV), is a reference to homosexuality. Since there are references to it in Egyptian literature (1500–1000 B.C.), its omission could not be because it was unknown. Considering all of the detailed laws in the Book of Leviticus, it is remarkable that it is nowhere mentioned. Possibly God did not want to lay a burden on us that was too heavy to bear.

Before masturbation is dismissed as a harmless release of sexual energy, we've got to contend with Peter's warning, "Beloved, I urge you as aliens and strangers to abstain from fleshly lusts, which wage war against the soul" (1 Peter 2:11). Paul taught that we should keep our minds from thinking evil. "Finally, brethren, whatever is true, whatever is honorable, whatever is right, whatever is pure, whatever is lovely, whatever is of good repute, if there is any excellence and if anything worthy of praise, let your mind dwell on these things" (Phil. 4:8).

Even when practiced infrequently, masturbation is accompanied by sexual fantasies which fall under the general category of lust or covetous desire. Those who are told it isn't sinful may experience less guilt but still admit that it makes them have a sense of shame or at least defeat. Interestingly, though other kinds of sexual behaviors are talked about freely in our society and some people may claim without shame that they live immorally, masturbation still causes a sense of embarrassment. Walter and Ingrid Trobisch published their correspondence with a girl named Ilona who was struggling with the practice. She wrote, "On the surface masturbation is something beautiful for me which I want to experience. But deep down it is a burden. Every time that I give in I feel guilty even though no one ever forbade me to do it" (*My Beautiful Feeling*, InterVarsity Press, p. 26). Masturbation involves taking a gift designed by God to establish an intimate relationship with another person and using it selfishly. It's aborting the development of a caring and communicating relationship.

For some, the habit leads to enslavement. Though it may be a temporary release of sexual tension, it can eventually inflame the passions. Sometimes it's like using oil to put out a fire. Some practice it several times a day unable to be free from its grip.

Excessive masturbation is often a symptom of a deeper problem which may not be sexual. Sensuality grows best in the soil of a self-indulgent life: overeating, oversleeping, avoiding difficult challenges, etc. It may also be symptomatic of deeper unresolved spiritual problems.

For example, a person who is angry because he believes he has been shortchanged in life may masturbate telling himself, "Considering what I've got to put up with, I deserve this little bit of pleasure." It then becomes a compensation for the discouragements of life, and one's dependency on it grows. As Ilona wrote, "Usually deep down, there is a feeling of dissatisfaction with one's self and with one's life, which one tries to overcome in a short moment of pleasure. But one does not succeed. The desired satisfaction is not reached" (*My Beautiful Feeling*, p. 18).

If an individual is angry with God, his partner, or his job, these issues must be faced before masturbation can be over-come. If not, he will not only lack the desire to change but take the path of least resistance and fall back into the habit. It's that "What's-the-use-anyway?" feeling that tends to dampen any motivation for change.

When the Bible says that the power of sin is in the Law, it implies that we are under sin's dominion because of its condem-nation. As long as there is a sense of defeat or self-hatred, it's hard to keep up the fight.

Because our sexuality is so intimately connected with the very core of our being, masturbation generates shame as well as guilt. That's why it can become such a major stumbling block in our spiritual growth. And the more it becomes the focus of the mind's attention, the more powerful it seems to become.

Although in one sense all sin is sin, there's no doubt that some sins are greater than others. Christ condemned the Phari-sees because they tithed but neglected the weightier matters of the Law (Matt. 23:23). Self-righteousness is more heinous to God, but because it isn't linked to sexuality, it may generate little guilt. Yet such sins of the spirit are even more abhorrent to God than the sins of the flesh. Not for a moment should we excuse sensual sins, but sometimes we lose our perspective when we're in the midst of the struggle.

The answer then is not to condone masturbation. It seems unlikely that it can be done in faith, believing that God ap-proves—and Paul taught that whatever was not of faith was sin. Rather, it must be considered as a fleshly habit that God wants the person to overcome, even if it takes a period of time before abstinence is realized.

As for the guilt, there is an excellent cure. The conscience can be cleansed and one can be at peace with God even while he/she struggles.

No one *has* to masturbate. Because the sex drive is so power-ful we are tempted to let our passions lie to us and get away with it. The tendency in our time is to avoid the suffering of temptation. We are programmed to take the path of least resistance, but there are alternatives that help reduce the frequency of this sexual practice, if not eliminate it all together. The interval between times can become greater, and God stands by to help and to forgive.

Getting a Proper Perspective
Many Christians are disappointed when God doesn't immediately answer their prayers to be freed from this habit. But sometimes they are praying for the impossible: they are expecting God to take away their sexual desires; but usually He does not do this. The desires themselves are God-given, though if we give in to them too frequently they may become more intense. God wants to teach us how to overcome temptation rather than remove the temptation completely by neutralizing our sex drive.

In fact, we must thank God for the temptation (notice I didn't say the sin). Like one man said, "I told God I would thank Him even if I was tempted until the day I died." Such a life of thanksgiving will help you view your struggle with objectivity and perspective. A person who struggles with masturbation is often so preoccupied with his struggle that he cannot view himself objectively. A life of praise helps us stand back and realize that God has a purpose in all things.

If you are struggling with masturbation I suggest that overcoming it should *not* be your highest priority. If so, you will be discouraged if you fail. Instead, determine that your goal in life is to become an intimate worshiper of God. This will help give a proper focus to your life. If you seek first the kingdom of God and His righteousness, victory will eventually be added to you (see Matt. 6:33). To be an excited Spirit-filled Christian is your ultimate goal. If in the process God grants you complete victory over this sin, fine. Yet if you struggle with it don't let it deter you from your desire to know God better.

On a given day you may feel no lust and believe that finally you have overcome your temptation. But then suddenly you are ignited and you find yourself burning with desire. Later you may be surprised and wonder how this could have happened. Of course, we can never assume that any habit that once controlled us has vanished for good. But it's particularly important to surrender to God every day whether we think that we will be tempted or not.

What if you lack the desire to stop? Maybe you think that you deserve this secret pleasure and besides, you think that you could never overcome it anyway.

Mary V. Stewart told about her struggle, "I eventually stopped—again, not without struggle and stumbling, but I stopped. I wanted God's Spirit more than I wanted transient physical titillation, and over and above that, I began to see that abstinence made sense in terms of optimal preparation for *real* sharing with a *real* person" (*My Beautiful Feeling*, p. 116).

Of course God is patient, for He knows that sexuality is rooted in your very being. He may be working on you in other areas, bringing your life in line so that you continue to grow even though you're struggling. But eventually He will close in; He will patiently prod you to give up the toys of the heart. Best of all, you'll be motivated to face the underlying issues that may have contributed to your decision to resign in defeat. But you will not be released from this habit as long as you look within, trying to find out whether you're victorious. Within the human heart is every evil desire; the potential of sin is forever with us. It's faith in the Lord Jesus Christ and what He has done in our behalf that should be our greatest desire.

Let me suggest some basic steps to help overcome temptation:

1. Confess and forsake any sin that may be the cause of your temptation. Pornography, sensual television programs, or any other stimulants should be avoided. In 1 John 1:9 we read that

God does two things for us: He cleanses us and He forgives us. Both must be received by faith. But the cleansing process means that we are totally honest before God and willingly obedient in staying away from those things which draw us into sensuality.

Remember that this will not put an end to the temptation itself for sin arises within us. As James wrote, "But each one is tempted when he is carried away and enticed by his own lust" (James 1:14). But even so we can control many of the outer stimulants.

2. You must accept yourself and your circumstances. If you are single thank God for that, even though you desire marriage. If you are upset with God because He has not given you a partner, you will likely never overcome your temptation. It's this feeling of "I deserve this pleasure because I've been short-changed" that causes a person to give up in the struggle. God has a right to do as He wishes with His own, and unless we accept that, we will fail in our struggle against sin.

Satan's desire is to make us unhappy with our lot in life. Someone has said that marriage is like the flies on a screen door: those that are out want in and those that are in want out! At any rate, few people are satisfied.

God wants us to be content even when we have desires that are unsatisfied. God has to teach us that there's more in life than sexual fulfillment.

Remember the story of the potter and the clay? Paul wrote that the clay does not have the authority to tell the potter what to do. The clay must submit to the potter, accepting whatever decisions the potter makes on its behalf. When we can accept God's will for us and particularly distressing circumstances as from His hand, we'll be in a better position to say no to temptation and yes to Him.

3. Believe that God through Christ has won a victory over sinful passions. That's tough to believe because people ask, "If that is so, why am I driven by these desires?" This will be the

greatest test of your faith: will you believe your passions or will you believe God? I'm not implying that victory is automatic—simply that the ground for it has been laid in Christ.

We all have to learn that when we aren't walking in personal victory our faith vanishes. Of course it takes time to build faith. Paul prayed that "the eyes of your heart may be enlightened, so that you may know what is the hope of His calling, what are the riches of the glory of His inheritance in the saints (Eph. 1:18). Memorizing Romans chapters 6 to 8 will help us engraft the Word of God into our lives and build faith.

For those who find themselves driven by masturbation, perhaps practicing it several times a day, there may have to be a renunciation of satanic powers. Demonic spirits capitalize on our weaknesses, inflaming the passions. This can be done by submission to God and then saying, "Begone, Satan, for it is written. . . ." Then quote verses of Scripture that assure you of your position in Christ. James has given us this promise, "Submit therefore to God. Resist the devil and he will flee from you" (James 4:7).

4. Remember, the easiest time to resist temptation is the moment that the fantasies crop up in the mind. That's when the decision is to be made because it will never get any easier. As the thoughts continue to fester in the mind, and the passions are aroused, then masturbation may become inevitable. It's developing sensitivity to the Holy Spirit that helps us.

Yes, there will be failures in the struggle. But God also understands that we are sexual creatures, and He knows how intense the battle can become. So we must be secure in His acceptance of us and know that even when we sin as believers we are still "accepted in the beloved One."

Begin now to develop habits that will lead you to a fully committed life. God is with you each step of the way.

Study and Application

1. Develop the habit of getting out of bed in the morning when you awaken. Or else recite Scripture and pray, thanking God for the night's rest. To lie in bed is to invite lustful thoughts that appear to be under your control, but may soon not be.

Then spend 5 or 10 minutes with God. Submit yourself to Him fully. This may take several moments—ask God to show you those matters in your life that you may be withholding from Him. Spend enough time so that you know your new day is in the hands of God.

2. Memorize such verses as Ephesians 1:22; 2:4–6; 3:20–21. The Word of God cleanses the mind and gives the confidence to face temptation (John 15:3).

3. Choose beforehand how you will respond to sexual thoughts. Quote verses (Matthew 5:8, for example) five times consecutively. This doesn't guarantee that you will resist temptation, but if you are submitted to the authority of the Word, you'll in turn be able to exercise authority over your thoughts and actions.

4. Before you go to bed at night ask God to cleanse your mind and protect it from sensual thoughts.

5. When you fail, claim instant forgiveness. Don't delay even an hour. God does not find it difficult to forgive you. You may find it difficult to come to Him simply because you are so disappointed in yourself. But God forgives so completely; He never says, "Oh, no, not *you* again!" Even our constant need of confession is used by God to teach us the wonder of His grace.

8

My Friend, the Homosexual

The issue of homosexuality must be included in any discussion of sexuality. Time was when the matter could be dismissed on the grounds (probably mistaken) that only a few people exhibited sexual desire toward their own sex. Today it is different. Many people, including genuine Christians, find themselves driven by passions over which they seemingly have no control.

The term *homosexual* applies to either men or women who display sexual desires toward their own sex, though often the word *lesbian* is used to designate a female homosexual. Unfortunately, other descriptive terms such as weird and queer are frequently applied to homosexuals. Such language only contributes to deepening the wedge between homosexuals and heterosexuals (those who are attracted to the opposite sex).

Christians may think they have never met a homosexual, not realizing that some within the Christian church may be afraid to reveal their sexual orientation.

Sometimes homosexuals are stereotyped. We can't always recognize a homosexual by the way he dresses or speaks. Nor is it true that all homosexuals prey on children. Though this

happens, the number who molest children is probably no greater than the number of heterosexuals who molest children.

We also have been guilty of misunderstanding the depths of
feeling connected with homosexuality. Superficial comments
such as "Why doesn't he get married?" are hurtful because they
reveal a shallow understanding of what a homosexual thinks and
feels. Meeting and counseling homosexuals dispels these mis-
understandings. If we would take time to understand the pain
and sense of rejection that homosexuals endure, we would be
more sympathetic. They have the same need for love and respect as anyone; in fact, they are often more sensitive persons.

Imagine yourself in the position of a homosexual: You are a
male 18 years of age. You have a powerful erotic attraction to
men. You have not consciously chosen this lifestyle. At puberty
your desires were already directed toward the same sex. Your
friends are attracted to girls, but you are not interested. The
pressure of society and your feelings remind you that you are
abnormal, your peers call you weird. You try to change but you
cannot. You implore God for help, but your passions continue
unabated.

What would you do?

Tell your parents? They might not understand. In fact, one
organization established to help the parents of homosexual
children is called the Spatula Club—parents need to be
scraped off the ceiling when they hear the news of their child's
homosexuality!

Tell your pastor? Not if he's the kind who berates homosexuals from the pulpit. You have no idea what he may say to you.

As a result, the common response for the homosexual is to
find others with whom he can identify. He will probably seek
acceptance among those who share his viewpoint. If he's a
Christian, he might seek to defend himself, even to the point
of reinterpreting the Bible to make his lifestyle acceptable to
God and to others. If he's not a Christian, he may seek his

identity with radical "gay" organizations which are intent on changing laws to make homosexuality as respectable as heterosexuality. Gay groups believe that every school should have a practicing homosexual as a teacher so children can grow up viewing homosexuality as an acceptable alternate sexual preference.

Many homosexuals have been driven to these responses because of the insensitivity of the church. They are bitter because they feel that Christians don't take time to understand them. Consequently, some have written off the church and have sought their identity elsewhere.

No one should speak about homosexuality without a caring heart. I doubt whether anyone has ever changed by simply hearing a sermon against it. The teaching of Scripture must be accompanied with understanding, patience, and love. David Augsburger has wisely said, "It is so much easier to tell a person what to do with his problem than to stand with him in his pain."

This doesn't mean we reinterpret the Bible to suit the contemporary mind-set. It does mean that we try to understand homosexuals and listen to what they say, feel the pain of rejection that they experience before we comment on their lifestyle.

What Does the Bible Say?
The Scriptures teach that homosexual activity is sin. In the Old Testament a number of offenses were punishable by death. Among them were adultery and homosexuality. Specifically, God says, "If there is a man who lies with a male as those who lie with a woman, both of them have committed a detestable act; they shall surely be put to death. Their bloodguiltiness is on them" (Lev. 20:13).

In Romans 1:26–27 we read that homosexuality is against nature. This means that the homosexual is fighting against the nature of his own body. This is confirmed by Paul's use of the words *exchanged* and *abandoned*. It means that the homosexual has abandoned what his body naturally craves. Associated with this are guilt and fear which often drive the person to pursue further homosexual relationships. When Paul says that "God gave them over" it means that God delivers a person over to sin by intensifying the guilt in the individual's life. At this point the person will either come to complete repentance, or he will be driven more intensely by his passions. Paul speaks of the homosexual as "burned in his own lusts." This describes the consuming fire of homosexual passion.

Some evangelicals say that homosexuality must be accepted as an alternate sexual preference. They make a distinction between homosexual acts—which result from a conscious choice on the part of the individual—and homosexual orientation. Those who take this view believe some are born with homosexual tendencies and therefore are not guilty of personal sin and are not responsible for their "preference."

There is a difference between homosexual behavior and homosexual lust, as there is a difference between heterosexual lust and behavior, but this should not make us think that such desires are normal.

Dr. George Rekers writes, "All homosexual lust is abnormal and fights against normal sexual adjustment. Each instance of homosexual lust conditions the nervous system to an even stronger responsiveness to homosexual stimulation" (*Growing Up Straight,* Moody Press, p. 24).

The Bible is consistently clear: both homosexual acts and attitudes come under the condemnation of God. It is a perversion of God's will for man. It may be natural for someone to be a kleptomaniac, but it is nevertheless a perversion of God's will for man. Even homosexuals themselves admit that their desires and behavior are contrary to nature.

I'm not denying that homosexuality may be an unconscious adaptive step taken as a child, but even when this is the case, we can make choices which change our behavior. Ruth

Barnhouse, a Christian psychotherapist, wrote, "The process of psychotherapy entails a very large element of helping the sufferer to understand that he is not a victim of something beyond himself, but that choices made in the past, however unconsciously, can be reviewed and new decisions taken."

Homosexual desires cannot be excused because some grow up with them and they are therefore "natural." I know of no evidence that homosexuality is communicated genetically. Rather it is the result of environmental factors usually coupled with specific experiences that make a child vulnerable to the redirection of sexual passions.

What Causes Homosexuality?

We must resist the tendency to think that every homosexual fits into a neat stereotype, but there is no doubt that some general patterns emerge when we try to identify the cause of homosexuality.

First, there is the family. According to Rekers, "The fathers of homosexual sons are most often described as being aloof, hostile, and rejecting. More than four-fifths of adult male homosexuals report that their fathers were physically or psychologically absent from their homes while they were growing up" (*Growing Up,* p. 68). These men did not have a good male role model; consequently, their own sexual identity became confused; they simply could not relate meaningfully to the opposite sex. Often a passive or absentee father accompanies an overprotective, dominant mother in the home. The boy thus identifies with his mother, and assumes her sexual role. One man told me, "My mother dressed me in girls' clothes. At school the kids said, 'He must be queer.' I thought that they must be right, and I began to think about my identity. Soon I was attracted to other males."

If a mother hates men and communicates this to her son, she may make the boy vulnerable to homosexual temptations.

Particularly in the absence of a man in the home, the boy might begin to shrink from the male role that he should identify with. No one can calculate the amount of damage that hostility between parents contributes to the confusion of sex roles.

Child abuse also contributes to the reversal of sex roles. If a girl has been molested by her father, she may develop an aversion toward men which may drive her into lesbianism. To quote Rekers again, "Certain kinds of families can leave a child with unresolved emotional conflict or with feelings that tempt him to pursue a shortcut to intimacy by having sexual relations with a person of the same sex" (*Growing Up,* p. 67).

A second cause is sexual exploitation. Almost all children are at some time sexually stimulated by the same sex. For most, it is a fleeting experience. But if those feelings are exploited, they may persist and develop into a homosexual lifestyle. Psychologists tell us that at the age of puberty, a child is particularly impressionable, and if he or she begins to focus on the same sex, homosexual desires are intensified. Understandably, homosexual pornography can contribute toward a homosexual lifestyle.

Or a child can be introduced to homosexuality by an older man or woman who desires the child for sexual relationships. This may cause the child to withdraw from normal relationships, and feelings toward the same sex will then intensify. Many who have had such a homosexual experience mistakenly believe that they are doomed to grow up that way. What began as a onetime experience, ends up becoming a fixed pattern of thought and behavior. Rabbi Akiba is quoted as saying, "At the beginning (sin) is like a thread of a spider's web, but in the end it becomes like a ship's cable."

We've heard it said that someday God will judge America because we have sinned against such great light. I've often wondered why we don't have severe earthquakes or famine. Actually, America is already being judged with a punishment much more severe than these natural phenomena. The final judgment of God on Israel was the scattering of families (Deut. 28:32, 64). The emotional consequences of divorce on children are much more severe than a natural disaster could ever be. Little wonder God's last Old Testament word to mankind regarding the coming of John the Baptist (Matt. 17:13) included these words, "And he will restore the hearts of the fathers to their children, and the hearts of the children to their fathers, lest I come and smite the land with a curse" (Mal. 4:6).

With the breakup of our homes and harsh and unloving attitudes of parents toward each other and their children, it is not surprising that we have so many who feel the pangs of rejection and hurt. As a result, we have those who are driven by their inner torment to sinful relationships in an attempt to soothe the anxiety, fear, and bitterness that are latent in their hearts. This explains why homosexuality is increasing.

Whether they realize it or not, homosexuals are hurting persons. They've been so deeply wounded that they are more aware of the attitudes and feelings of others. They often disassociate themselves from Christians for fear of being rejected again. Unfortunately, this often means that they are quick to take up an offense and to harbor bitterness.

For those who admit their need, we ought to provide support and encouragement. Who among us has never been bound by sin which was brought on by the failures of those who have influenced us the most? Homosexuality is one of many consequences of our fallen world.

Is There a Way Out?

Christians are divided on whether or not Christ actually changes homosexuals into heterosexuals. Because many revert to homosexuality after extensive counseling, some feel we should have a less ambitious goal. The most we can expect, they say, is to teach them to resist temptation. Once an alcoholic, always an alcoholic; once a homosexual, always a homosexual in basic

preference, they say. Then they will not be involved in homosexual activity, even though they still will have homosexual
desires. The reasoning is this: Since all of us must say *no* to lust,
it really doesn't matter whether our lust is homosexual or
heterosexual. In either case, the same biblical teaching applies:
"Do not let sin reign in your mortal body that you should obey
its lusts" (Rom. 6:12).

Though such an approach may be laudable, I believe that God
is able to take a person *beyond* that to an actual redirection of
his or her sexual desires. When Paul discussed various kinds of
sinners, he included homosexuals, "And such were some of you;
but you were washed, but you were sanctified, but you were
justified in the name of the Lord Jesus Christ, and in the Spirit
of our God" (1 Cor. 6:11). He assumed that Christ had *delivered*
these people from their preconversion lifestyles.

Of course it's not easy. The homosexual who is a believer
should not think that God doesn't love him; nor should he conclude that he cannot grow in his faith even while he struggles.
I have met those who have displayed the fruit of the Spirit even
while they have regarded their condition with sorrow and contrition, but are yet unable to change. They are fellow-pilgrims
en route to the heavenly city.

With care, I would like to suggest for homosexuals some
basic processes, each of which takes time. One step may blend
into another, or need to be repeated, but I believe Christ is able
to deliver from *both homosexual desires and actions.*

Repent of sin without any self-justification. If you're asking
why you must repent for desires you didn't consciously choose,
think of it this way: If you were born into a family that was
greatly in debt, the responsibility for payment would be passed
on to you. Even though you had no choice in the matter, you
as the heir, would be expected to pay.

I don't think that any of us are fully repentant *until we realize
that we are held responsible for our inability to obey God.* God holds

us responsible even though we are by nature children of wrath. Grace is never poured out until we come to that point of full contrition and humility.

David learned, "The sacrifices of God are a broken spirit; a broken and contrite heart, O God, Thou wilt not despise" (Ps. 51:17). There can be no excuses, no appeals to our genes, or to our environment. We must take full responsibility for every attitude and every choice. The homosexual must renounce his lifestyle, just as a drunkard or an idolater must renounce his.

Uncover hidden bitterness. Often homosexuals have deep-seated fear and bitterness toward members of the opposite sex. Even when they won't admit these feelings, further probing usually reveals unloving attitudes (if not outright bitterness) toward a member of the opposite sex, either within or outside the family.

There may be even deeper bitterness toward those who have wronged the homosexual. Since homosexuality grows in ruptured family relationships, it's easy to see why such feelings may be deep-seated and difficult to uncover. Sometimes, they go back to infancy. Those who wish to study one counselor's experience in helping homosexuals to probe beneath the surface of their feelings may want to read *Broken Image* by Leanne Payne (Crossway Books).

Find a support person or group. One girl struggling with lesbianism wrote, "Good listening ears were few and far between. I desperately needed people who would listen to me—for hours on end at times. I didn't want pat answers. They were usually much too simplistic or naive to be helpful. I needed someone who would listen with God's patience and compassion." We all need a fellow believer with whom we have acceptance. In fact, habits can only be broken when we are accountable for our actions. Without friendship and accountability, there can be no deliverance.

Don't become discouraged. Remember, all of us struggle with something. We are learning to tear down the strongholds of the imagination through meditation on Scripture, and through full acknowledgment of our sin. Meanwhile, any believer who walks in submission can be a blessing and a testimony to others. We must depend on God's grace even during temptations.

Remember that God does not reject us as persons. It is important to feel loved by God and by others so that there can be a sense of wholeness, a feeling of well-being despite homosexual desires. This feeling may come gradually, for sometimes it is difficult to accept the idea that God loves us. It's important not to blame God, but to put aside bitterness. As long as we call His goodness into question, we are defeated.

One homosexual explained his course of action to me. He learned to look to God and praise Him when temptations came. He also memorized more than 200 verses of Scripture, and eventually God did change his desires.

Submission to God is the key. When we do this, we will be willing to accept whatever struggles we may have without the bitterness that intensifies them.

Finally, there must be a renewing of the mind. This happens only by learning the principles of spiritual warfare. We've got to know who we are in Christ before we can with confidence say *no* to temptation.

Study and Application

1. Paul said that those who were formerly homosexuals were now washed, sanctified, and justified (1 Cor. 6:11). Study these three words and state how they can be applied to our situation today.

2. Paul says that all of us are "by nature children of wrath" (Eph. 2:3). Since we are all accountable for our corrupt

natures, does this not imply that we are responsible even for that over which we have no control? How does this apply to those who have had homosexual urges since puberty.

3. Those who engage in homosexual activity "receive in their own persons the due penalty of their error" (Rom. 1:27). What do you think that penalty might be?

4. Read Philippians 4:4–9. What hints does Paul give about how to think pure and good thoughts rather than evil ones?

9

The First Step to Freedom

"Tell me man to man: is there a way out or isn't there? If there is I want to know about it; if there isn't, I'm going to blow my brains out."

This was the cry of a desperate man caught in the vice of sexual sin. He was a practicing homosexual, overwhelmed with a sense of guilt, tired of his secret liaisons, weary of making promises that he could not keep.

Where does he begin? Precisely where all of us must begin. We must know that we can be forgiven and have a new beginning. We must settle our past before we can get on with our future because the sin that condemns us is our master. If we feel guilty and polluted, and are filled with self-hatred, we are doomed to continue as a slave of sin.

Can you identify with what William Justice has written?

For every failure to live up to some *ought,* there is the tendency to punish one's self in such a manner as to produce another failure! And every failure produces the response, I ought not to have failed! ... Having failed, I punish myself in such a manner as to produce a further sense of failure. My cycle is complete only to begin again. I have failed to live up to an *ought* for which I feel guilty. Convicted of guilt I feel the need to pay. To pay, I choose a method that will leave me with a sense of having failed ... on and on rolls the cycle downward. It may be compared to a snowball rolling downhill, adding to its load and momentum with each revolution. The load of guilt that is picked up becomes greater and greater and the rate of descent becomes faster and faster. This cycle of the damned goes round and round and down and down and has the potential of going on and on eternally. That is at least one aspect of hell! (*Guilt and Forgiveness*, Baker Book House, p. 105)

Time does not obliterate the guilt. Guilt is not simply a feeling to unlearn. It's not the result of a repressive society. It is our God-given response to moral failure. No escape through drugs, sex, or diversionary pleasure can erase its pollution. Unless we are forgiven and cleansed, we'll give up and say, "I've already messed up, why shouldn't I do it again?"

Fortunately, God has an excellent remedy for guilt—forgiveness of sin because Christ in His death atoned for our sins.

An atheist asked Billy Graham, "If Hitler on his deathbed had received Christ, would he have gone to heaven, whereas someone who lived a good life but rejected Christ would go to hell?" That is a trick question. It was asked to make the Gospel appear ridiculous. But the answer is *yes*. If Hitler trusted Christ, God could forgive him completely because Christ's death included all of Hitler's sins! God values Christ so much that He can accept Hitler if he comes to God on the basis of Christ's merit, but He cannot accept a good man without Christ's merit!

In Zechariah 3 we read that Joshua, the high priest, was being cleansed by Jehovah while Satan watched, making accusations. Why was Satan so interested in Joshua's sin? It wasn't because he was concerned about Joshua entering heaven with filthy garments. Satan was angry that God was able to clothe a sinner with clean robes. Satan wanted Joshua to stay in his polluted clothes.

Christ is able to cleanse us despite the protests of the devil and our polluted consciences. Spurgeon wrote:

> Stand where you are; for remember, you are standing in the only place where pollution can be washed away, you are standing before the angel of the covenant. It is before Christ that sin is to be confessed. Confess it anywhere else, your sorrow is not repentance but remorse. "What is remorse?" says one. Remorse is repentance made out of sight of Jesus; true repentance is sorrow of sin in the presence of Christ. Foul and filthy as you are, there is but one voice which can speak you clean. Go not away from that voice. There is but one hand which can touch you and make you pure; stand where that hand is close to you, and still, filthy as your garments are, shun not the face of your best, your only friend, but breathe out this prayer, "Lord, if Thou wilt, Thou canst make me clean. Purge me, O purge me now, for Thy love's sake" (*Treasury of the Bible, Old Testament*, Vol. 4. Zondervan, p. 760).

Have you ever wondered whether your forgiveness is complete? Or maybe you've doubted whether you have genuinely repented? Repentance is not a change of mind (as many believe). It is a change of *direction*.

The Scripture is very clear. "If we confess our sins, He is faithful and righteous to forgive us our sins and to cleanse us from all unrighteousness" (1 John 1:9).

Confession Means Repentance

The word *confess* literally means "to agree together with." Confession must go with repentance. Both words indicate a wholehearted submission to God, along with an admission of the evil of sin. To use grace as an excuse for our behavior falls short of full agreement.

A Christian medical student decided to give his wife an abortion. He knew it was sin, and prayed before the operation, "O God, forgive the sin I am about to commit and guide my hand." Unfortunately, his wife died of complications that came as a result of the surgery. He was only halfhearted in his agreement. Though we must never add conditions to the free grace of God, we must remember that confession means that we withhold nothing from Him. It is full agreement.

Psalm 51 is an example of true confession. David had to remind himself of the compassionate attributes of God or he might never have come for pardon and cleansing. He began by saying, "Be gracious unto me" (v. 1). The Hebrew word means "to give undeserved favor." He was asking for a gift he didn't deserve. David appealed to God's loving-kindness, His "unfailing love" (v. 1, NIV). The word loving-kindness has the same root as the word *stork,* the large bird which builds its nest high in treetops and which is known for its unfailing loyalty to its young (that's why the stork is associated with the birth of a baby). Then he mentions God's great compassion. David was thinking of the compassion a mother has for her helpless baby who can do nothing to care for itself. She doesn't abandon it.

God has emotions and can be touched by our feelings of helplessness and of failure. He does not turn His back on us. Rather we turn our backs on Him. We don't have to persuade Him to accept us; we need only turn around to receive His grace.

We can sense the completeness of David's submission. He's not asking God to help him work himself out of a mess. David leaves it all up to God, and is satisfied with whatever God does.

A fully repentant person does not come to God with an agenda. There's no attempt to bribe God or to make heroic promises to do better next time. Self-justification gives way to self-abhorrence.

Job spent many hours complaining about God's treatment of him. But when he finally saw God, he forgot his well-rehearsed speeches. "I have heard of Thee by the hearing of the ear; but now my eye sees Thee; therefore I retract, and I repent in dust and ashes" (Job 42:5–6, KJV).

As long as we cling to some particle of goodness in ourselves, we have not fully repented. If there are thoughts about keeping our options open—if we think we just might want to sin again—we have not come to full agreement.

The price is further bondage.

Admitting Rebellion against God

We go to great lengths to cover our sin. One man in love with another man's wife kept a device on his telephone to detect whether or not his phone was being tapped. We use lies, deceptions, and playacting to keep sin hidden.

Secrecy is the name of the game.

What delusion!

Our sin is against God, the supreme Lawgiver. David uses three words to refer to his immorality—*transgressions, iniquity,* and *sin.* All of these imply an absolute standard. He had sinned with a clenched fist.

David underscored his rebellion, "Against Thee, Thee only, I have sinned, and done what is evil in Thy sight" (Ps. 51:4). We're tempted to say, "Wait a moment, David. You sinned against Bathsheba and you killed Uriah—that wasn't exactly a private act between you and God." But David saw that sin is first of all against God. We hurt others, but sin is rebellion against the Lawgiver. If a child disobeys his parents who tell him not to touch the vase on the mantle, and the ornament crashes to the floor, and his baby brother steps on the broken glass, disobedience to his parents is the basic issue. Whether his baby brother was hurt is secondary.

If Bathsheba had not become pregnant, David would not have killed Uriah, but his relationship with God still would have been ruptured. Whether or not the consequences of sin become evident to others makes little difference to God.

A Christian couple who had premarital sex were disturbed when they thought the girl was pregnant. Their agony was relieved when a physician told her she wasn't pregnant after all, and the couple went to an exclusive restaurant in Chicago for an evening of celebration. They were elated that their fears were groundless. *That is not repentance.*

A girl who gets an abortion may feel guilty because of what she did to the unborn baby yet be oblivious to what she has done to God. That is halfhearted agreement.

"All things are open and laid bare to the eyes of Him with whom we have to do" (Heb. 4:13). Things that are done in secret are going to be proclaimed from the housetop. Shame will no longer be hidden. In heaven secret sins are already public. Dr. Lewis Sperry Chafer said, "A secret sin on earth is an open scandal in heaven."

A woman in South America brought her dirty laundry to the river. She was so ashamed of her dirty clothes, that she didn't want to take them out of the basket in the presence of other women. So she dipped the entire basket of clothes into the water several times and then took them back home. Sometimes that's the way we confess our sins. We admit them to God very quickly and in one big bundle. We are not honest with God, or the people around us.

John White wrote, "We have a choice to make when we come to God about our sin. Either we justify ourselves, or else we justify God. We cannot do both. If I am right, then God is wrong. If I say, 'You would be wrong to condemn me altogether because I cannot really be held responsible' and so forth, I am challenging the righteous judgments of God. Whether I realize it or not, I am putting God in the wrong" (*Daring to Draw Near*, InterVarsity Press, p. 56).

Are you still softening the full force of your sin? Are you calling adultery "an affair"? Are you pleading that you have certain needs which God ought to take into account? If so, you are not agreeing fully with God.

One man had the habit of looking at pornography in drug

stores. He never bought, but he liked to browse, just to keep up with the latest. He'd confess his sins, and be restored to fellowship, but a few weeks later, he would be looking again.

One day he realized that he didn't really think of what he was doing as evil. He had been confessing his sins only because he felt guilty; not because he had offended God. When he realized that his actions were done in the presence of God and that God might discipline him by letting him become ensnared in sensuality, he developed a healthy fear of his secret practice.

"After that, I never let myself touch it because I was afraid of what God might bring into my life. I no longer considered it a viable option."

Like a recovered alcoholic who can't afford the risk of one glass of wine, this man finally admitted that pornography was evil and he could not trust himself with it. Knowing that it was an invitation to slavery, he let God take it out of his life completely. Jesus said, "Do not sin anymore, so that nothing worse may befall you" (John 5:14). Do you see the error of reasoning, "If I sin in a big way, I can be forgiven in a big way, and experience God's grace in a big way"? God might let you be enslaved in a big way and may even let your heart be hardened in a big way.

Taking Responsibility for Sin

Five times in the first three verses of Psalm 51 David uses the word *me* or *my*. He didn't blame Bathsheba, though she was also guilty—what was she doing bathing on a rooftop in the evening sun? David said, "Behold, I was brought forth in iniquity, and in sin my mother conceived me" (v. 5). We are born under the judgment of God.

David didn't use his sinful nature as an excuse. In Philadelphia someone scribbled on a wall "Humpty Dumpty was pushed." The message was that nobody is responsible for what he does. It's environment or genes.

We're tempted to say God's standards are too high, that He is mocking us by setting up a standard He knows we cannot reach. We must remember that God has reached down to help us. Augustine said, "O God, demand what You will, but supply what You demand." Through Christ we can be forgiven and be accepted by God.

Agreeing with God means that we have no excuses left. We come defenseless into the presence of God with no objection to whatever God wants to do. Tozer wrote: "God rescues us by breaking us, by shattering our strength and wiping out our resistance. Then He invades our natures with that ancient and eternal life which is from the beginning. So He conquers us and by that benign conquest saves us for Himself."

Accept Cleansing as well as Forgiveness

Yes there is a difference. It's possible for a person to be forgiven and yet feel polluted. David prayed, "Wash me thoroughly from my iniquity, and cleanse me from my sin" (Ps. 51:2). Cleansing is the subjective application of forgiveness. Forgiveness is what God does *outside* of us. Forgiveness has to do with our legal standing in the sight of God; when He forgives us, we are credited with Christ's righteousness. Cleansing is what God does *inside* purifying our minds and consciences.

If we have come to Christ for forgiveness but still feel guilty, our feelings will catch up to our theology when we insist on cleansing. Once we have confessed a specific sin, we do not confess it again. Cleansing is ours by faith.

A polluted conscience smothers the joy and gladness that Christ came to bring us. David knew that the problems his sin caused could not be straightened out, yet he could sing for joy. He wanted to be so clean that the stain would be gone forever.

Fresh snow comes down from heaven without any visible impurities. It can be so white it nearly blinds the eye, and yet David prays that the Lord would make him "whiter than snow." Isn't that gracious of God?

Almost every satanic attack is directed toward our consciences. Evil spirits desire to make us feel foul, dirty, and beyond hope. Such feelings of self-hatred cannot be met by trying to convince ourselves that we are really beautiful people. Rather, we've got to admit that there is no good thing within us; we have no inner resources to meet such an attack. By depending on Christ we are washed, and that's where sin's power loses its grip.

Psychiatrists are trying to put people to sleep with drugs when God might be wanting to keep them awake with a guilty conscience! When we are cleansed, we are at rest before God and ourselves.

Accept God's Discipline

A sure way to tell whether a person is fully repentant is his attitude toward discipline. Not one of us likes to have our sins exposed, but if they are, we must accept it without complaint.

The difference between David and Saul is found in their attitudes when they repented. Saul said, "I have sinned; but please honor me now before the elders of my people" (1 Sam. 15:30). That kind of confession can be said a thousand times without attracting the mercy of God.

David also said, "I have sinned," but there was no struggle to maintain his reputation or even his position as king. Later when he was forced to leave Jerusalem, he asked that the ark of God be returned to the city. "If I find favor in the sight of the Lord, then He will bring me back again, and show me both it and His habitation. But if He should say thus, 'I have no delight in you,' behold here I am, let Him do to me as seems good to Him" (2 Sam. 15:25–26).

A woman who was upset because she was disciplined by the church complained about the treatment she received. She gossiped about the elders and what they had done. Such an attitude betrays a lack of repentance. A person who is broken because of his or her sin will submit to discipline, even if it's unjust. It is received as from the Lord. As long as one pleads for special treatment, as long as there are attempts at self-justification, the repentance is incomplete.

No act of adultery ever became as publicized as that of David! For 30 centuries millions have read about David's sin. His prayer of repentance was not only recorded, but it was sung in the temple. What irony that a man who tried to cover his sin should have had it so widely exposed.

I'm not suggesting that all sexual sins should be made public, but when we fully agree with God we no longer attempt to cover our sin. "He who conceals his transgressions will not prosper, but he who confesses and forsakes them will find compassion" (Prov. 28:13). A repentant man submits his reputation to God and trusts Him to do "whatever is best in His sight." Richard Roberts wrote that a person is repentant "when fear of exposure and shame so long dreaded will now be thought as nothing in comparison with the prospect of cleansing and renewal."

Submission to discipline also means agreeing to make restitution. Maybe all that we can do is humble ourselves, asking the forgiveness of those we have wronged. Without a spirit of contrition, we are still harboring rebellion in our hearts.

We may not be able to ask another person for forgiveness, or it may be unwise; but if we sincerely ask the Lord, He will show us the way.

A Clean Slate

The Old Testament distinguishes two kinds of sins. One is a sin of passion, the kind that is committed on the spur of the moment. Another is a sin of defiance or "sinning with a high hand." David committed both kinds of sin. It took Uriah four days to come to Jerusalem, and he was in Jerusalem three days before he went back to the battle. David had a long time to think about his plot to kill the soldier. It was sin with a high hand.

Furthermore, adultery and murder were sins for which there was no sacrifice. Both were to be punished by stoning. That's why David said, "For Thou dost not delight in sacrifice, otherwise I would give it; Thou art not pleased with burnt offering" (Ps. 51:16, KJV). There was no restitution for these sins. David could weep night and day and live with remorse until he died, but Bathsheba's purity would never be restored nor would Uriah be brought back to life. Yet David found forgiveness because he cast himself helplessly before a gracious God.

Have you met people who have committed sins for which there is no restitution? I know a Christian man who is tormented with the thought that he fathered a child and that somewhere his girlfriend is having to raise that child by herself.

Then there is a couple who gave up a child for adoption. After they were converted to Christ, they discovered that their baby had been placed in the home of a couple who belong to a religious cult. They have to live with the thought of their child not having a Christian upbringing.

A man had developed the art of seduction and introduced young women into prostitution. He had fathered a number of children through his liaisons. Can a man like that be forgiven?

We all can be forgiven and cleansed. If we attempt to wash ourselves, we are still filthy, but when God washes us, we are clean.

If we say that God can forgive us but we can't forgive ourselves, that is devilish pride. Do we require more than God? Do we really have a right to withhold forgiveness when God Himself, the pure and the holy One, has granted it? Remorse is nothing more than trying to face our sin apart from Christ.

In John 8 we read about a woman who was caught in adultery. The Pharisees wanted Christ to stone her, and He consented, inviting them to be among the first to cast stones. When they couldn't do so because of their own sins, He turned to her and said, "Neither do I condemn you; go and sin no more."

Someone has said that God casts our sins into the depths of the sea and then puts up a sign which reads "NO FISHING."

"The sacrifices of God are a broken spirit, a broken and contrite heart, O God, Thou wilt not despise" (Ps. 51:17). These are the first steps to freedom from sensuality.

Study and Application

1. A clear example of halfhearted repentance is that of King Saul. Study these passages, and find out why Saul fell short of "full agreement" with God (1 Sam. 15:24–31; 24:16–22; 26:21–25; 28:6–25).

2. Read Job 40:1–5 and 42:1–6. What did Job have to repent of? What are some of the characteristics of his repentance?

3. Read Daniel's prayer of repentance (Dan. 9:3–19). What additional insights does he add to our understanding of repentance?

4. The Book of Judges can be summed up in the cycle of repentance and chastisement in 2:11–23. What were the steps in this cycle? What disciplines did God impose? How does this apply to us?

10

Christ Can Change Us

"Every renewed soul is the scene and stage, wherein the two mightiest contraries in the world, spirit and flesh, that is, light and darkness, life and death, heaven and hell, good and evil, Michael and his angels and the dragon with his, are perpetually combating hand-to-hand," says Puritan writer John Gibbon (*Puritan Sermons,* Vol. 1, Richard Roberts Publishers, p. 98).

We all have been irritated by someone who in all seriousness expects us to do the impossible. It's like telling someone who is depressed to "Cheer up!" as if emotions can be turned on or off like a faucet.

The Bible is filled with seemingly impossible commands. "Do not let sin reign in your mortal body that you should obey its lusts" (Rom. 6:12). Paul wrote as if we can simply say, "OK, lust—you can do whatever you please, but I'm not going to obey you anymore. No more fantasies, pornography, or mastur-bation—that's it!"

Who hasn't said, "Never again" to some sin, only to come back to the point of having to say it again.

Is Paul giving us an impossible command? Is God mocking us

by giving standards that are beyond us and then berating us for falling short? Mark Twain expressed anger toward God for giving to each human being a source of joy and pleasure, then forbidding its use until marriage and restricting it to one partner.

Are some of God's commands impossible? Think of the words of Christ to the man who had been sick for 38 years. Jesus said, "Take up your pallet and walk" (John 5:11). The man might reasonably have replied, "Heal me first, and *then* I'll walk!" But he didn't say that. In faith he obeyed and God took over from there. The sick man was asked to do the impossible, and to his astonishment he could!

Take the command, "Do not let sin reign in your mortal body that you should obey its lusts" (Rom. 6:12). Paul recognized that this inclination to lust lies in every human heart. How can we make sure that it doesn't *reign* there? Enablement comes with the command. Regardless of our excuses and rationalizing, Paul wouldn't command us to turn away from lust unless he thought such freedom is possible for every believer. *Everything God asks us to do is based on what He has already done* to make victory possible for us. Jesus' work on the cross has provided us with forgiveness of sin and a way to God, and the Holy Spirit within gives us power for living. God's standard is high, but His power is available to use against lust or any other sin. A thorough understanding of God's provision for us is necessary to fully apply it in our lives.

Understanding the Cross

We receive two benefits from Christ's death. We're better acquainted with the first than the second. Do you remember when you realized that forgiveness is not based on good works—that Christ's death made a complete sacrifice to God for sins? Jesus paid my whole debt to God. On the cross Jesus said, "It is finished." That means paid in full.

Have you ever counseled someone who believes that salvation is a cooperative effort between man and God? Good works and faith are needed, the argument goes. Such theology breeds uncertainty. We can't be sure our part is enough; and what is more, the Bible teaches that God doesn't accept our righteousness. Because Christ's work is complete, our responsibility is to believe (Eph. 2:8–9). The New Testament teaches that Christ not only paid the whole debt, but *He also won the full war.* His provision for us did not end with His sacrifice for us. In Colossians we are reminded of His continuing work. "Having forgiven us all our transgressions, having cancelled out the certificate of debt consisting of decrees against us and which was hostile to us ... He has taken it out of the way, having nailed it to the cross. When He had disarmed the rulers and authorities, He made a public display of them, having triumphed over them through Him" (Col. 2:13–15).

We must not be misled because Satan is still on the loose and rebellion is rampant. Because people are shaking their fists at God and doing whatever they please, we might get the impression that Christ's victory was not decisive.

The outcome is never in doubt. He is far above all rival powers. "He [God] has raised Him from the dead, and seated Him at His right hand in the heavenly places, far above all rule and authority and power and dominion, and every name that is named, not only in this age, but also in the one to come. And He put all things in subjection under His feet" (Eph. 1:20–22).

This means angels, demons, and nations. God tolerates rebellion because He has graciously chosen to postpone judgment. He is waiting until the world is on the brink of self-destruction; then He will return to rule as King of kings and Lord of lords. All legal questions of His authority and power are settled; Christ will rule the world.

We have to be firmly convinced that Christ is the Mighty

Conqueror, to visualize Him seated in heaven; His work finished. The battle is over. He is representing His people before God.

What difference should this make to us who struggle with the two-steps-forward and three-backward routine? We know Christ is victorious, but He seems far away from our personal struggles.

The good news is that all believers are personally identified with Christ's victory. More than 100 times Paul refers to us as being "in Christ." We are even seated with Him at the right hand of God the Father (Eph. 2:6). We have two addresses: one on earth; the other in heaven. We have been delivered from the domain of darkness and transferred to the kingdom of His beloved Son (Col. 1:13).

If we grasp these facts, we know we don't have to obey our passions. We can participate in Christ's authority over them. If this weren't true, the commands in the New Testament would be impossible for us to keep. God would be expecting the impossible. Just as He knows we can't forgive our own sins, He knows we can't free ourselves from their power either. Andrew Murray wrote, "Remember that however much you abhor what is revealed of self within, and however much you long to be delivered from it, no effort on your own, no self-abhorrence or self-crucifixion will bring the slightest relief. It is God who must do it."

Paul repeatedly exhorts us to holiness, not because we can change our character on our own. We can let God do it because we are "in Christ" and that position can affect our practices.

Read Paul's epistles and you will be impressed with the number of commands he gives that are firmly rooted in our position in Christ. In Romans, for example, we read of being baptized into Christ, participating in His death and resurrection. Because of what God has done He can give the command, "Even so consider yourselves to be dead to sin, but alive to God in Christ Jesus" (Rom. 6:11). Or Paul's statement, "If then you have been raised up with Christ" becomes the basis for a whole list of commands including, "keep seeking the things above, where Christ is, seated at the right hand of God" (Col. 3:1) and "consider the members of your earthly body as dead to immorality, impurity, passion, evil desire, and greed, which amounts to idolatry" (3:5).

In some cases Paul spends whole chapters telling us who we are in Christ before he gives specific demands regarding Christian living (Eph. 1—3). The reason we can say *no* to the flesh is not because of how we feel, for our feelings fluctuate, nor because we've had a good time with the Lord in devotions this morning, for some mornings we don't. Nor is it because we've been a Christian for 20 years. It's not even because of the depth of our own yieldedness. It's certainly not because we've become tired of failure and resolved to do something about it. That's like thinking that an elephant could fly if he really got serious about it. The reason that we can obey Paul's commands, is because of what God has already done for us in Jesus Christ.

If Christ, who is our Head, is in heaven and we are members of His body, doesn't it follow that we also have access to the Father and "sit" at God's right hand? Sin is under our feet too!

Using Our Authority
I used to ponder Paul's words, "For sin shall not be master over you, for you are not under law, but under grace" (Rom. 6:14). I couldn't understand why being under grace means that we are free from sin's power. Then I realized that under the Law we would have to serve God in order to be blessed. Under grace God blesses me first, and then enables me to serve Him. We can obey from a position of strength.

Let me illustrate this.

In St. Louis an unmarried woman and an older married man were living together. She felt guilty and angry about the relationship. When a friend suggested she move out immediately, she replied, "I can't do that . . . I own the apartment!"

She had asked her live-in companion to leave, but he wouldn't budge. He threatened that if she insisted, he'd "get even." They had lived together for more than a year, and he argued that he had a "right" to the apartment, whether they were married or not.

The woman ignored his threats and went to an attorney to get a court order that he be evicted. He ranted and raved. She even needed police protection because she was so terrified. When he finally left, she had the locks in the apartment changed. And though she's still frightened, she is on her way to spiritual and emotional recovery.

What gave a 115-pound woman the courage to evict a 200-pound man? *The law was on her side.* In the final analysis, the man had no rights, regardless of how loudly he shouted.

All of our legal battles are taken care of; we have a right to evict the enemy (the flesh and the devil) from the premises. These enemies don't leave peacefully. They argue, lie, and threaten. They remind us of all the benefits we'd receive if we'd just let them alone. They even make promises to change, but they won't leave. Even when they are forced to go, they try to contact us again to see if we are ready to compromise.

We can say *no* to the flesh. Our enemies have been defeated. Faith commands them in the name of Jesus to leave, despite their protests. Unless we know who we are, and understand our rights, we will say, "I've tried to change but can't." Even yielding ourselves to God, important though that is, won't be of much help unless we are firmly convinced that God enables us to say *no* to our passions. In Christ we have won the war.

Because Christ had people like us in mind when He died, His power can be applied to anyone. Our passions may be unusually powerful, but that's no reason why we must be under their authority. It's not a matter of becoming stronger so that we can master them. Strength comes not by resolutions, but by faith in Christ's victory. If we compare our desires to the power of God, we can take heart. There is hope.

When Hudson Taylor learned to depend fully on Christ he made the startling discovery that it didn't matter where he was or how great his difficulties were. After all, God had to meet Taylor's needs, and therefore whether they were great or small was really irrelevant. "It little matters to my servant whether I send him to buy a few cash worth of things, or the most expensive articles. In either case he looks to me for the money and brings me his purchases" (*Hudson Taylor's Spiritual Secret*, Moody Press, p. 163). We have resources equal to any emergency. Dealing with our passions is not impossible.

Failures may come if we resist Christ's authority. We may do fine for a while, but without continual dependence on Him we will fail.

Understanding the Holy Spirit

Before we were converted, we may not have sensed any conflict within us. Perhaps we fulfilled our desires as we saw fit. When we trusted Christ as Saviour we received the Holy Spirit. The Spirit confronts the power of the flesh. Paul speaks of this conflict, "For the flesh sets its desire against the Spirit, and the Spirit against the flesh; for these are in opposition to one another so that you may not do the things that you please" (Gal. 5:17).

Paul precedes this description of the conflict by an important statement: "But I say, walk by the Spirit, and you will not carry out the desire of the flesh" (Gal. 5:16). That's a promise we can sink our teeth into. Regardless of how strong our desires may be, they are not as powerful as the Holy Spirit. If we walk in the Spirit, there's no way our passions can rule us.

Paul stressed the need to cooperate with the Holy Spirit in freeing us from the power of the flesh. "If you are living according to the flesh, you must die; but if by the Spirit you are putting to death the deeds of the body, you will live" (Rom. 8:13). If then we understand the power of the Holy Spirit, we will resist temptation and be out of the swamp of moral slavery. "The fruit of the Spirit is love, joy, peace, patience, kindness, goodness, faithfulness, gentleness, self-control; against such things there is no law" (Gal. 5:22–23). There it is: *self-control.*

Many Christians know that the Holy Spirit has power, but for them walking in the Spirit is reserved for missionaries, pastors, and mystics. The power of the Spirit is beyond the grasp of ordinary Christians. Most of us reason backward. We think that if we could be more victorious over the flesh, God would reward us by giving us the fullness of the Holy Spirit. So we struggle, hoping that someday we will be good enough to experience the Holy Spirit's power. But Paul would say we've got it backward. We are not given the Holy Spirit as a reward for fighting against the flesh, but as a Helper to fight the flesh successfully. A defeated Christian needs the Spirit's power now—not five years down the road. It's given to every child of God.

How can the Spirit's power be released? There are two basic requirements: First, we are not to grieve the Holy Spirit (Eph. 4:30). Paul lists a whole catalog of sins that must be confessed so that the Spirit is not hindered in His work. The Holy Spirit is sometimes represented by a dove, a bird that is particularly sensitive and gentle. We must take inventory and ask whether there are sins that have not been "put away." Second, the Spirit's fullness must be received by faith. Christ invited people to come to Him and drink, "He who believes in Me, as the Scripture said, 'From His innermost being shall flow rivers of living water.' But this He spoke of the Spirit, whom those who believed in Him were to receive; for the Spirit was not yet given, because Jesus was not yet glorified" (John 7:38–39). The giving of the Spirit depended on the ascension of Christ. Christ's work on the cross is the reason why God can forgive us; His Ascension is the reason why the Spirit can fill us.

How can we bring this into our experience? We may feel unworthy of the Spirit's power, or think there will be a more convenient time, but if we have received the forgiveness of the Cross, we can receive the power of the Ascension.

F.B. Meyer tells of his experience. "I left the prayer meeting and crept away into the lane praying, 'O Lord, if there was ever a man who needs the power of the Holy Spirit, it is I. But I do not know how to receive Him, I am too tired, too worn, too nervously run-down to agonize.' Then a voice said to me, 'As you took forgiveness from the hand of the dying Christ, take the Holy Spirit from the hand of the living Christ.' " Meyer continued. "I took for the first time and have kept on taking ever since."

The Need for Faith

God wants us to believe Him rather than our emotions. Sure, Satan influences our feelings, but we must be able to hold on to the truth. The person of faith believes God even in the fluctuating circumstances of life. He goes on trusting.

One of the best illustrations of faith is that one of the 10 lepers who came to Christ for healing. Jesus told them to go to the priest that he might pronounce them healed. "And it came about that as they were going, they were cleansed" (Luke 17:14). They obeyed, never doubting they were healed.

How can we increase our faith? D.L. Moody said that for many years he struggled to have strong faith but it eluded him. Then he read "Faith comes from hearing, and hearing by the Word of Christ" (Rom. 10:17). He stopped praying for faith and began to spend more time in the Scriptures.

Our faith will increase when we learn to praise God for whatever happens in our lives. He still seeks worshipers (John 4:24). He is honored by a life of persistent praise and thanksgiving, "He who offers a sacrifice of thanksgiving honors Me" (Ps. 50:23).

You will find that your love for God increases while your love for pleasure diminishes. Just as we lose our desire for steak when we nibble on a candy bar, so the pleasures of the world spoil our appetites for God. He wants to give us a desire for Himself—and it happens when we are immersed in His Word. Grab hold of the promise that lust need not reign in your mortal body.

Study and Application

1. What do you think Paul means when he speaks of us being dead with Christ? (Rom. 6:1–7)

2. Give an example of how a person might "consider himself to be dead to sin" (v. 11).

3. What does it mean to become a "slave of righteousness"? (v. 18)

4. In Romans 8:13 we read, "by the Spirit you are putting to death the deeds of the body." What is our part in this process?

5. How would you contrast the works of the flesh and the fruit of the Spirit? (Gal. 5:16–26)

6. What practical steps can you take right now to apply to your life the victory that comes from the Cross and the Holy Spirit?

11

We Can Control
Our Thoughts

"Over the past three years my mind has become filthy. Thoughts that never used to enter remain with me now. I am obsessed and in my mind's eye I see people having sexual relationships. I can't help myself. Though I've prayed about my condition, prayer seems unreal to me; there is no real depth and I find it hard to focus my mind on God. I know God is merciful and I have no intention of frustrating His goodness and long-suffering toward me. My problem is my mind which seems to be beyond control. What do you think of my condition?"

This letter came to me from someone who heard a message I gave on the radio. Many people are obsessed by sensuality. For them, sexual purity seems to be impossible.

In Bunyan's classic work *Mansoul* the fortress was beseiged by strong, malignant forces, but the enemies couldn't take the fortress until its gates were opened from the inside. Remember the discussion of how the fortress eventually would be captured? Diabolus speaking to his cohorts says, "We'll cajole them, delude them, pretending things that will never be and promising things they shall never get. Lies, lies, lies—the only way to get

Mansoul to let us in. And so our intentions will be invisible and we will be invisible—that is, all except one of us" (*Chronicles of Mansoul,* Regal, p. 5).

Thus Satan got the human mind to cooperate with him and we've been reaping the consequences ever since. The strategy remains the same—lies, lies, lies.

We all know that battles are won or lost in the mind. The most important part of us is that which nobody sees—except God. If we could flash all of the thoughts we had last week on a screen, we'd have a pretty good idea of our spiritual condition.

The mind is particularly strategic because it works in conjunction with the brain. Thoughts are not physical; they are essentially spiritual in nature. This means that thoughts are not forced on us either because of the chemistry of the brain or the feelings of the body. Yet, we all know what it's like to be a slave to the mind. Jonathan Edwards would say that we have the natural equipment (mind, emotion, and will), but we lack the moral ability to think rightly. Every honest person agrees!

Because the mind is spiritual in nature, it exists in the same realm as God, angels, and demons. Little wonder it is the scene of incredible battles. We have our own lusts to contend with as well as spiritual forces that vie for our allegiance.

Paul wrote, "And do not be conformed to this world, but be transformed by the renewing of your mind, that you may prove what the will of God is, that which is good and acceptable and perfect" (Rom. 12:2). The key is to be transformed (the Greek word is *metamorphis*) rather than be pushed into the mold of the world. God wants to change our thought patterns so that our lives are conformed to the image of Christ.

Think what we are up against. By nature we have a "reprobate mind" (Rom. 1:28, KJV), a "blinded mind" (Rom. 8:7, KJV). In fact, Paul writes, "the mind set on the flesh is hostile toward God; for it does not subject itself to the Law of God, for it is not even able to do so" (Rom. 8:7). Accepting Christ as Saviour gives us a new nature, but often the old thought patterns continue.

If we are careless, Satan can put ideas into our minds as he did in the case of Ananias and Sapphira (Acts 5:3). Little wonder Paul describes the mind as a stronghold or fortress, and testifies, "We are destroying speculations and every lofty thing raised up against the knowledge of God, and we are taking every thought captive to the obedience of Christ" (2 Cor. 10:5).

What an encouragement to know that our stray thoughts can be captured and brought into submission to Christ! Then the Holy Spirit is free to work through our minds, to give us freedom from immorality. "The mind set on the Spirit is life and peace" (Rom. 8:6).

We can yield and surrender, beg and plead, but until our minds are renewed we will always revert to patterns of sinful thought and behavior. God has given us the equipment we need to dismantle the imaginations of the mind that we might be free to serve Christ. *Everything God asks us to do is possible because of what Christ has already accomplished.*

How is the mind renewed? There's no formula, but we've got to build some specifics into our walk with God. If we are consistent, we will find the promises of the New Testament completely reliable.

We Need a Worshipful Mind

We've got to begin with a proper understanding of God. Remember the adage: The smaller your God, the bigger your problem; the bigger your God, the smaller your problem.

We've learned that God has much at stake in our temptations. He was deeply grieved by David's sin. He had to scrap greater plans for David's future, and His name was blasphemed by the heathen.

If we want to think rightly, our first question is: Do I have a heart for God? Too often we want victory as an end in itself, but such freedom should be a step toward Christlikeness which is God's ultimate purpose. Fellowship with God is more important than victory over sin (though we need the latter to enjoy the former). God Himself must be first in our thinking when we talk about freedom from immorality.

Do I want to master my passions just so I can have a clear conscience, live a successful life, and raise a fine family; or am I fully committed to living for the praise of God's glory?

God lets us struggle so that in the end we will have a greater appreciation of Him. Too often we run away when we fail, hoping to hide from God as Adam did in the Garden. God is calling us even through our shame and our guilt. He's waiting for us to give up our toys and fully surrender our hearts to Him. He sifts us to separate the wheat from the chaff. He tests us to see where our loyalties really lie. When overcome with fierce temptation, which side do we take? Either way, God is the One with whom we have to deal.

A friend was so weary of lust that he prayed, "God, if I commit adultery I will disgrace Your name. Either take these thoughts out of my mind or strike me dead. I don't want to discredit You." At that point God, along with angels and any demons that might have been listening, knew that this man was fully submitted to God. That was the beginning of his freedom from unabated sexual cravings.

Are we that jealous of God's honor? Or do we want to be released from the torment of sexual temptation so life will be easier? If we are concerned only about ourselves, we are using God to our own ends. He becomes the means to our own clear consciences and wholesome self-images.

If we love God with mind, heart, and soul, we'll continue to worship Him even if He doesn't free us from our sexual frustrations. We have an obligation to keep that first commandment whether or not He does what we think He should.

We must ask ourselves the question: When we succumb to

temptation, what concerns us the most? Is it the guilt we experience, is it wondering whether anyone will find out, or the fact that we have grieved the Holy Spirit who is God? (Eph. 4:30)

Fellowship with God is the best deterrent for lust. One man writing anonymously in *Leadership* about his struggle with pornography said that all the negative arguments didn't work for him. The dire warnings about a failing marriage, guilt, or punishment did not prevent him from visiting strip joints and pornographic bookstores. Then he read a book by Francois Mauriac and his attitude changed. Mauriac concluded that there is only one reason to seek purity. "It is the reason Christ proposed in the Beatitudes: 'Blessed are the pure in heart for they shall see God.' Purity is the condition for a higher love—for a possession superior to all possessions: God Himself." The writer continued, "We are the ones who suffer if we sin, by forfeiting the development of character and Christlikeness that would have resulted if we had not sinned. . . . Here was a description of what I was missing by continuing to harbor lust: I was limiting my own intimacy with God" (*Leadership,* Vol. 3, #4, p. 43).

I think it was George Mueller who said, "The foremost duty of every Christian is to have his soul satisfied in his God." Here is the ultimate reason to surrender the control of our passions to God.

How much time are you giving to worshiping God? Is your fellowship with Him growing?

Think about Truth

Paul wrote about the Gentiles (the unconverted) as walking in "the futility of their mind, being darkened in their understanding" (Eph. 4:17–18). In Psalm 2 the writer asks, "Why are the nations in an uproar, and the peoples devising a vain thing?" (v. 1)

Modern man is filled with vain imaginations. The soaps, erotic literature, and movies have caused millions to develop powerful fantasies based on lies; namely, that man's way is better than God's. This flood of sensuality has ignited discontent and a callous disregard for the rights of others. No one is satisfied: A sexy wife would produce greater satisfaction; doing our own thing is more fun that being tied down to a family, and a life of ease is ultimate happiness. Responsibility is old-fashioned. Whatever feels best at the moment is what we ought to do.

Some are caught between two worlds: the reality of day-to-day existence, and the lure of the imagination where real happiness (supposedly) exists. The real world becomes dull and boring compared with the world of unbridled imagination. The beautiful girls in pornography make men dissatisfied with their ordinary-looking wives. The exhilaration of drugs and alcohol provides an escape from the realities of a humdrum existence. When the tension becomes unbearable, a man or woman abandons everything and takes the plunge into the fantasy world. A Christian woman said she had become so hooked on soap operas that she decided to have an affair. She thought, *There's a whole world out there that I'm missing*. Families are split, promises broken, and lives fractured—all because of lies.

Samuel Baker tells a story of Egyptian troops who were dying of thirst in the Nubian Desert. In the distance they saw what they thought was water, but the Arabian guide warned them that it was only a mirage. An argument erupted and the guide was killed. The whole regiment rushed toward the water. Mile after mile the thirsty troops trudged deeper into the desert as the glistening mirage led them on. Finally they realized that the lake they thought was there was burning sand. They died pursuing something that wasn't even there. A search party discovered their withered corpses.

Here are some of the lies that many believe today:

• God is unfair in giving us passions and then restricting their fulfillment.

• By careful planning, we can sin secretly without harm.

- A truly erotic pleasure is worth any discipline which God might impose as a result.
- We can live in the world of fantasy and still be committed Christians.

Once we have firmly rejected these lies, we must get on with meditating on truth. Christ prayed to the Father, "Sanctify them in the truth; Thy Word is truth" (John 17:17). We must meditate on Scripture day and night. God promises, "How blessed is the man who does not walk in the counsel of the wicked, nor stand in the path of sinners, nor sit in the seat of scoffers! But his delight is in the Law of the Lord" (Ps. 1:1–2).

It is practicing the principle of replacement. Jesus told a story of a man who had been indwelt by a demon. After the wicked spirit was expelled, it passed through waterless places, seeking rest. Finding none, it decided to return to its original abode, and to its satisfaction, saw that its original house was unoccupied, swept, and put in order (Luke 11:26). Though the man had been free for a time, he had not substituted something good in place of the demon. When the demon returned, it brought seven others more evil than itself and the man was worse off than before. It's important for our minds to be clean, but also to be filled with God's Word.

Feeding the Mind

God has always had trouble getting us to understand that our dependence on Him is moment-by-moment. That's why He told the Israelites they weren't to store manna in their tents (except on the day before the Sabbath). The sight of thousands of people kneeling on the ground searching for manna each morning was a reminder that they needed God's blessing *every day*.

Why was God so strict about this? Because He didn't want them to get to the point where they could survive on their own. He was giving them a lesson in dependence. Quite literally, they were between God and the deep Red Sea!

In the New Testament Christ is pictured as the manna that came down from heaven, "Truly, truly, I say to you, it is not Moses who has given you the bread out of heaven, but it is My Father who gives you the true Bread out of heaven. For the Bread of God is that which comes down out of heaven, and gives life to the world" (John 6:32–33). Christ invites us to receive spiritual food from Him. We must follow the pattern of getting it daily, as Israel did. Christians go to church assuming that they will receive enough blessing to last all week.

Our lives would be changed if we spent 20 minutes with God each day before 9 o'clock in the morning. Such discipline would keep us spiritually refreshed, and we would begin each day committing ourselves to God.

The greatest difficulty is in getting started. The second is to keep going!

Remember the story of the Indian who said he had a good dog and a bad dog within him? When someone asked which one is the strongest he replied, "The one I feed the most."

Some Christians have starved their new natures so much that they have lost all appetite for spiritual reality. It takes awhile to get it back.

The study assignments at the end of this chapter can help restore it.

Be Rude to Sinful Thoughts

Think of your mind as a castle, then determine what thoughts you should admit and which you should expel from the premises. When lust, greed, ungratefulness, and other enemies knock for entry, don't even give them the time of day. Treat them like you would a man who rings your doorbell at 2 A.M. Regardless of his sweet words, you're not in the mood to negotiate. Keep the door locked and take up the matter with your new landlord. Remember the scriptural advice, "Watch over your heart with all diligence, for from it flow the springs of life" (Prov. 4:23).

The greatest problem is to believe that these thoughts are actually sinful. You may intend to entertain them for only a minute but they weaken your defenses against another attack.

Sinful thoughts may reappear under a different label—as friends rather than as enemies. They will remind you that other fine Christians struggle with lust too—"it's part of being human." They also may encourage you to pity yourself—"you deserve a break today."

By now those thoughts aren't knocking on the door, they're pulling it off the hinges. Related thoughts gather to reinforce them and you realize you're about to be overwhelmed.

What shall you do?

Thank God for the temptation and view it as an opportunity to prove that Christ is stronger than the flesh. Recall that the Holy Spirit drove Christ into the wilderness to be tempted of the devil. God has allowed you to be brought to this moment because He's teaching you some lessons you couldn't learn otherwise.

Remind yourself that you are in Christ, seated above every principality and power. Because of what He has done you need not submit to this temptation. Anchor your soul in the assurance that these enemies have already been conquered.

Remember that your real struggle is not with the temptation but with God. Whether you say *yes* or *no,* He is the one to whom you are answerable. To some degree you're accountable to yourself and to others, but ultimately you report to God. The real question is: Will you believe Him?

Quote verses of Scripture that assure you of victory. You are fighting from a position of strength.

The flesh and Satan tell lies. They want to overwhelm you, and make you think that you have to obey your passions. In Christ, you don't!

Don't be put off by repeated temptations. Satan will try to wear down your resistance, but continue to submit your mind fully to God.

Long-range Effects

"But we all, with unveiled face beholding as in a mirror the glory of the Lord, are being transformed into the same image from glory to glory, just as from the Lord, the Spirit" (2 Cor. 3:18). Christlikeness comes when we behold in the Word of God the glory of the Lord. We are transformed as we meditate on Him as He is seen in the Scriptures.

I don't know how it happens; God does it. The adage says it all: "You're not what you think you are; but what you think, you are."

Remember Nathaniel Hawthorne's story of the great stone face? Some rocks on the side of a mountain had been thrown together in such a position as to resemble the features of a man. When the little boy Ernest inquired about the expression on the face, which was both noble and sweet, his mother told him a story that passed on from one generation to another: In some future day a child would be born who would be the greatest person of his time and he would resemble the great stone face.

Ernest never forgot the story. When a rumor spread throughout the valley that a man was coming who resembled the stone face, he was as excited as the other people in the valley. But Ernest was disappointed. The man was greedy, and his face didn't have the kindness of the great stone face.

Ernest spent every free moment gazing at the glorious features and yearned for the day when the right man would come to the valley. Other men appeared, but they never resembled the great stone face.

Ernest at middle age was thoughtful and generous. Neither his friends nor he, least of all, suspected that he was more than an ordinary man. By the time he was an old man he was full of wisdom and kindness. People came from far and near to talk with him.

One day a poet who had heard of Ernest came to the valley. Ernest listened to the poet and was so impressed that he thought that his new friend bore a resemblance to the beautiful features etched on the mountain. But the poet said he was unworthy of such an honor.

As Ernest addressed an audience gathered in the open air, the poet recognized that Ernest was the likeness of the great stone face he had gazed at for so long.

We will never be Christlike by trying to resist temptation, as necessary as that may be. We must fill our minds with the wonder of Jesus Christ and have an insatiable desire to be like Him. Then slowly, perhaps imperceptibly, we are transformed into the image of Christ. Our temptations which were so powerful lose their attraction when we become consumed with all that Christ means to us. Paul said "that I may know Him, and the power of His resurrection and the fellowship of His sufferings, being conformed to His death" (Phil. 3:10).

Study and Application

1. The best way to have our minds renewed is to memorize Scripture—daily. Read and reread whole chapters until the words and ideas are fixed firmly in mind—forever. Begin with Psalm 1, John 15:1–11; Colossians 3:1–11.

2. Using a concordance or *Nave's Topical Bible* find verses of Scripture which relate directly to other battles you may be facing in your life. Memorize these verses as well.

3. Learn to use your temptations as an "alarm system." As soon as certain thoughts enter your mind, reject them, quoting the Scriptures you've learned.

4. Spend 20 minutes with God before 9 A.M. every morning. During that time of prayer and Bible reading, claim God's promises for victory that day.

⌈12⌉
Resisting Satan's Strategies

"The nightmares I had become accustomed to over the years subsided; but a much more real harassment began to assert itself. Tinkering with the occult had been deliciously exciting, but when Christ entered the picture, Satan began to show his true colors—colors of fear, confusion, and doubt. The devil becomes angry when he loses a partner in crime. But with Jesus on my side the demon is like a roaring lion without teeth" (Terry Bradley, *Moody Monthly,* October, 1976, p. 130).

Any Christian who is serious about holy living will be in conflict with the devil, or more accurately with demons who are under the devil's control. People who have given themselves over to sensuality at some point in their lives probably will be overrun by evil thoughts and impulses. Because our sexual desires are so much a part of us, and because sexual purity is necessary for successful family living, we can expect that Satan will make sex a battleground. He will assure us that pleasure and companionship are available outside of God's prescribed will and that the consequences can be hidden.

Satan strikes, overwhelms, controls, and since he has no

moral scruples, he uses every imaginable form of deceit in his arsenal. Every believer is his sworn enemy. He promises freedom, but always enslaves; he tantalizes with pleasure, but always demeans.

• A woman whose mind is filled with sensuality says that she cannot sing hymns in church without giving the words a double (sexual) meaning, or read words from the Bible without sexual innuendos. Everything she sees is polluted.

• A father becomes sexually stimulated by his daughter who is scarcely two years old. He can't trust himself to be alone with her.

• A teenage girl had such compulsive sexual desires that she propositioned any man who approached her. When the police came to pick her up, she urged them to have sex with her.

• A Christian college student was arrested for public indecencies. He would expose himself as he walked down the street.

• A man desired (and had) sexual intercourse with animals. He could only think of sex between human beings in perverted and bizarre ways.

Many live with fantasies and passions they share with no one else for fear or rejection. They believe they are weird, different, and of no worth to God or man. One common misconception is that they have committed "the unpardonable sin." They are convinced that even God cannot tolerate them anymore. They hate themselves and believe that if God is righteous, He must surely hate them too. They live within the walls of their own prisons of fear, anxiety, and belief that they are beyond hope. They've tried to make promises to themselves and God, only to find that they repeat their behavior.

They desperately need to share their inner conflicts with someone who will accept them, but not their behavior. "What you need is to warm your soul in the sunshine of another person's respect and understanding, and in so doing begin to rediscover respect for yourself" (John White, *Eros Defiled,* InterVarsity Press, p. 144).

We derive our understanding of who we are from other people. If a vice lies hidden within us, and we fear telling someone, we will bear those burdens in the torment of loneliness. Sharing the need is necessary, but usually it's only a beginning. When we have given ourselves to persistent sin, we are engaged in spiritual warfare; Satan needs direct confrontation. First consider how we can resist him and weaken his grasp on us.

Satan's intense interest in us is not because he thinks we have intrinsic value. He would like to destroy us and would do so instantly if God didn't prevent him. He wants to ruin us so that he can get back at God. He hates us with the same passion he hates Christ. If we succumb to sin, saying, "That's just the way I am," Satan gloats.

Looking at His Strategy

Here are some of the more common methods that Satan uses to beguile us and lead us into sin.

He works undercover. Satan and the wicked spirits he controls stay in the background so they are not easily detected. Like plain clothes detectives they prefer to work unrecognized. Satan's goal is to have us serve him, while we think we are serving ourselves. His suggestions are passed onto us so deftly we think they are our own.

His first "cover" is the flesh. "The deeds of the flesh are immorality, impurity, sensuality, idolatry, sorcery, enmities, strife, jealousy, outbursts of anger, disputes, dissensions, factions, envying, drunkenness, carousing, and things like these" (Gal. 5:19–21). When we struggle with sensuality we generally attribute it to the flesh, but demons use the flesh to intensify our desires. That's why it's not always possible to distinguish between the works of the flesh and the works of Satan, they blend into one.

Demons watch us and then concentrate on our most

vulnerable weakness. They wear one of a dozen different masks that correspond to the works of the flesh. They'll take fleshly desire and pervert it, inflame it, and make us think "we were born that way." Along with magnified desires comes guilt, and the mind is preoccupied with a sense of helplessness. A good word for this is *obsession*. Satan doesn't care whether it's pornography, adultery, homosexuality, or other forms of sinful thoughts and behavior. As long as the Holy Spirit is grieved, and joy has drained from our lives, Satan is on the winning side.

A second form of disguise is the human mind. Wicked spirits can inject thoughts into our minds, and again we are led to believe that these ideas (usually rationalizations) are our own.

Ananias and Sapphira lied about the amount of money they received for a piece of property. Covetousness kept them from being straightforward. They saw a perfect opportunity to be well thought of in the church and at the same time to keep a nest egg for a rainy day. Why not tell a white lie?

They did not have to sell any of the property, as Peter so clearly told them (Acts 5:4), but they wanted to be honored, and after a thoughtful discussion agreed to lie.

Peter asked, "Ananias, why has Satan filled your heart to lie to the Holy Spirit?" (v. 3) They were not aware that Satan was personally present in their home; they never dreamed that he had planted the suggestion in their minds hoping they would pick up on it. As far as they were concerned it was nothing more than their decision.

The New Testament teaches that Satan is involved in situations such as a fear of witnessing for Christ (Luke 22:31–32); adultery (1 Cor. 7:5); holding a grudge (2 Cor. 2:10–11); and evil betrayals (John 13:27). In these and a hundred different situations, Satan and his hosts are actively planting lies in the human mind.

"So then the devil made me do it!" you say. Not quite. He gave you the idea, but you chose to run with it, and for that choice God holds you responsible. Adam and Eve tried to blame one another, and even blame Satan. It was he who tempted Eve to eat. What does God say? He says each must bear the consequences of rebellion (Gen. 3:14–21).

Satan's strategy is to inflame the desires of the body and plant rationalizations in the mind. Because of these disguises, we often are completely unaware that we've been duped. We are like the soldier who sits in his barracks, refusing to believe the reality of war even while his building is being shelled.

He causes spiritual blindness during temptation. Satan not only injects ideas into our minds, but causes us to be blind to sin's consequences. At the moment of temptation we can forget verses of Scripture; we won't remember the guilt, anxiety, and tears that follow sexual sin. Christ said that Satan snatches seed of the Word of God from the human mind (Mark 4:15). Peter did not remember Christ's prediction that he would deny Christ until after the rooster crowed.

A man who met an unusually enticing woman in a bus depot was so carried away by her charms that he found himself asking her to meet him in a motel room. "I didn't even know what I was saying . . . I couldn't have cared who was watching or whether we'd get caught—only one thing mattered."

In Proverbs there is an apt description of such an experience. The one who is seduced by a harlot follows her "as an ox goes to the slaughter . . . until an arrow pierces through his liver; as a bird hastens to the snare, so he does not know that it will cost him his life" (Prov. 7:22–23). An animal cannot think beyond his perceptions. He thinks neither about God nor tomorrow. Only his immediate desires matter. When spiritual truths are pushed out of our minds, we act like animals. "I don't know why I did it. It's just not like me—it was so stupid!"

No one was ever lured into alcoholism by seeing a drunk staggering along a street covered with his own vomit. Nor is one led into adultery by seeing broken homes and weeping children. Such consequences are often out of view. As Christ said to the Jews who had rejected their Messiah, "[These things] have been hidden from your eyes" (Luke 19:42).

Deception then is the devil's chief weapon. Satan wants to deceive us and have us believe we are just "doing our own thing."

Satan skillfully uses the art of the slow approach. Often Satan strikes suddenly but he uses the slow approach with those who are committed Christians. He moves us from the familiar to the unfamiliar. He gives us time to rationalize, to make excuses as to why we want to see a particular person, or be in a certain store where pornography is sold. He is gratified when we sin in our minds, and have no harmful effects, because he likes us to believe that we can handle our own sins when we really become serious about them. He's not so much concerned about whether our sin is big or little as he is about our perception of sin itself. The little sins will eventually become big as long as we think that we, in ourselves, are able to contain them.

A con artist in the city of Chicago persuaded a businessman to give him $5,000 for an investment. At the end of three months the man returned $10,000 to the investor. He repeated the same tactic, always careful to give the investor a high rate of return. Trust was developed between them and one day the con man asked for $50,000 and got it. That was the last time they met!

Remember Samson? His weakness was women, particularly the women of the Philistines. He said *no* to Delilah three times before he gave in and told her the source of his strength. Mark it well: Satan doesn't care how many times we say *no* to temptation as long as we stay in the vicinity of it! Eventually he'll get us.

Time is on his side. Give him an inch today and he's prepared to wait five years before he gets his mile. The process of sin is never static, it must move backward or forward because no compromise is possible. Even if the pendulum moves back and forth, Satan is satisfied. Someday when we're dozing we will fall into his well planned trap.

What shall we learn from the slow approach? Even if we are victorious today, we can't be sure of future victories. The sense of self-confidence and well-being that we have today can drive us down the path of destruction tomorrow.

Satan works through guilt. He tries to get us to feel so defeated that we give up the idea of moral resistance. He prefers that we either feel no guilt whatever, or be burdened with excessive guilt. Most Christians want to feel guilty when they fall into sin. After all, they want to prove to themselves that they are morally sensitive, and guilt is a testimony of their relationship with God. Some people, however, feel guilty for not feeling guilty. Like one man put it, "I expected God to rain judgment from heaven when I walked into that X-rated movie. Yet I went to work the next day as usual, the sky didn't fall in. It's been a few weeks now and I've still not confessed my sin because I don't feel as bad about what I did as I thought I would. I suspect I'll do it again."

Paul talks about seductive spirits who lure people away from the truth; "seared in their own conscience as with a branding iron" (1 Tim. 4:2). The *Chicago Tribune* carried a story of a man jailed for committing more than 20 rapes. Despite the terror he caused these women (one of them attempted suicide later) he said he had no guilt until after he was arrested. He did it without a twinge of conscience.

The opposite side of the coin is excessive guilt. Some persons are convinced that they are too terrible for God to forgive. They are running away from God, thinking that He would prefer to see them dead. Unfortunately, they consider themselves to be unworthy of God's grace. So as long as they hate themselves, Satan has won a victory. If you feel overburdened with guilt, he will get you to believe you are beyond forgiveness. If you don't feel as guilty as you should, he will get you to believe you lack appropriate sorrow for your sin. Either way, you will be kept from God's grace.

He inflames resentment against God. Back in the Garden of Eden, Satan accused God of being evil. He implied that God didn't desire the best for Adam and Eve. Satan uses the same strategy today. Many people (including Christians) rise up in rebellion against God, arguing that God is unfair in giving them sexual desires and then expecting them to conform to His narrow laws. A woman who enjoys sexual fulfillment lives with a husband who is impotent. Isn't it only right that she find a man who can appreciate her physical beauty and give her the satisfaction she craves? Or what about the single person, caught in a web of loneliness and seeking the intimacy that would meet the desires planted within every human being? One writer puts the rationalizations of the world in these words: "We end up with sex drives that virtually impel us to break rules God laid down. Males reach their sexual peak at age 18, scientists tell us. In our culture, you can't even legally marry before then, so when a male marries, if he has remained chaste, he has already forfeited his time of greatest sexual prowess.... Couldn't our hormones or chromosomes have been arranged so that mates would more easily find satisfaction with just one partner? Why weren't we made more like animals, who, except for specified periods, go through their daily routine (nude to a beast) with hardly a thought of sex. I could handle lust better if I knew it would only strike me in October or May" (anonymous, *Leadership Magazine,* Vol. 3, No. 4, 1982).

Resentment against God is seen when homosexuality is considered normal. The argument is that it's unfair to ask someone to give up his sexual preference, and that is an implied questioning of God's justice. If we can't bring our passions into line with God's will, the contemporary move is to fulfill our passions and say that we are fulfilling God's will anyway.

Satan exploits bitterness. I believe many people should "forgive God." He needs no forgiveness, but they must bury resentment and submit to His authority. As Christ taught those who complain against the inequities of life, "Is it not lawful for Me to do what I wish with what is My own?" (Matt. 20:15)

The cause of Satan's downfall was rebellion, and some of that poison has fallen onto every human heart. When we become angry with God, we are taking sides with Satan. He delights that we are agreeing with him.

The Way to Freedom

Recognize Christ's Authority. Unfortunately the ascension of Christ is often thought of as an article of the creeds. In the New Testament the Ascension is presented as positive proof that Christ has conquered every enemy. In Ephesians we read of Christ, "He [God] raised Him from the dead, and seated Him at His right hand in the heavenly places, far above all rule and authority and power and dominion, and every name that is named, not only in this age, but also in the one to come. And He put all things in subjection under His feet, and gave Him as Head over all things to the church" (1:20–22).

Christ is seated at the right hand of God. The Old Testament priests stood at the brazen altar offering sacrifices. They never had a chance to sit down because their work was never completed. But Christ sits; the victory has been won. Also, Christ is not merely above all principalities and powers but *far* above them. The symbolism is obvious: His victory wasn't even close; the outcome was never in doubt. He won decisively and with finality. His foes are now His footstool. The nations may rage and take counsel against the Lord but "He who sits in the heavens laughs, the Lord scoffs at them" (Ps. 2:4). Satan can rant and rave; he can threaten and demean; he can seduce and deceive, but his humiliation is already history. In a matter of time he will be exposed for what he is and be thrown into the lake of fire forever (Rev. 20:10).

Christ's position at the right hand of God the Father denotes high honor. He has ready access to the Father and is assured of unqualified acceptance. Christ crushed the head of the serpent and the devil knows it.

How can we reconcile the fact that believers are in Christ and share His victory with the fact that Satan makes such deep inroads into their lives?

First, we must apply Christ's victory by faith; that is, regardless of our temptations there must be a firm insistence that Christ has indeed triumphed. Even then, victory isn't automatic.

Christ gave the disciples authority over all demons yet later the disciples confronted a demon that would not respond to them. Christ rebuked them for their lack of faith and added that some do not come out except by prayer and fasting (Matt. 17:21). God wants to teach us that faith must be built up in our hearts, and triumph can never be thoughtlessly assumed.

God lets us struggle with Satan to teach us about the nature of sin and our own weakness. If our successes were always instantaneous, we'd begin to think, *Sin isn't so bad after all. I can enjoy it and be forgiven whenever I like and get out of it without a hassle.* Spiritual conflict is a means of God's discipline to let us know how destructive sin can be.

If an Israeli soldier wanders into Arab territory (or vice versa), he's in for a long struggle. He may plead that it happened in ignorance or without harmful intent. No matter. He can appeal on the basis of his citizenship, but he's not going to be returned without the scars of battle. He'll have learned a powerful lesson about where the boundaries are and where he ought to take his "vacation" next year.

Those who are victimized by compulsive sensuality usually know where they have crossed the line whether through incest, pornography or extramarital sex. Sometimes they've walked deliberately into Satan's territory, the world which lies in his power (1 John 5:19). They want to be free, but they are struggling.

The first step is to know that Satan's defeat is already accomplished. Visualize Christ seated at the right hand of God with His enemies beneath Him. Then see yourself with Christ.

Renounce Sin. Sometimes we underestimate the intensity of the conflict with our passions. We think that victory comes by simply knowing who we are in Christ and then confidently facing whatever comes along. But our enemy tries to use our pasts as a launching pad for his attacks against us.

The admonition "Do not give the devil an opportunity" (Eph. 4:27), could be translated, "Don't give the devil a place of dwelling." We are not to give him any reason for thinking that he can continue to control us.

When persons enter another country illegally, it's often difficult to have them deported, especially if they've lived there illegally for a number of years. They insist that they've earned the right to continue there. We must resist Satan and renounce those practices that have put us on his turf. Here are some sins that must be renounced in the name of Jesus Christ:

• Occult practices, such as fortune-telling, the Ouija board, astrology, palmistry, ESP, and reading horoscopes. Ask God to bring to mind those involvements that may give Satan license to harass you.

• Sensual practices, such as alcohol, drugs, illicit sex, mind control, and pornography.

• The influence of others over you. The second commandment says that God allows the effects of idol worshipers to continue in a family until the third and fourth generations (Ex. 20:5–6). Those who are in false cults often have fallen into idolatry. Renounce any influence which may have come via your ancestors or even those who have been trying to help you while themselves being under satanic control.

Sometimes God instantly delivers a person from compulsive

behavior and thoughts. At other times, it's a slow, steady process. Though God gave the Israelites the whole land, He told Joshua that the enemies would be driven out, "little by little" (Deut. 7:22).

The question is whether we are willing to completely repent of all sin and willingly submit to whatever discipline may come as a result of disobedience. If we know who we are in Christ, we have a *right* to be free from moral slavery.

Keep Up the Conflict. Often a believer will resist Satan with great success and think, "At last, I'm free!" That's a dangerous moment. A sense of self-confidence, even when it appears to be God-directed, can set us up for another fall. When that happens, Satan will make us think that victory isn't worth the price. He will make sure that we remember the pleasure of sensuality without being able to recall the sorrow that accompanied it. When we find ourselves back at square one, we think, *There's nothing to it after all . . . just as I suspected!*

But if Satan attacks us a hundred times, we are to resist a hundred times. Christ was harassed three times in rapid succession. Resisting Satan is not something we do twice a week; it's whenever we find our minds being drawn away to former lusts. We must develop sensitivity to the first promptings of the Holy Spirit. When the enemy overwhelms us, we must say, "I reject this thought in Jesus' name."

That doesn't mean that the battle is over. Desire may even intensify. Satan's goal is to throw us off balance by creating unbelief in our hearts. He'll suggest a hundred different reasons why the Scriptures don't really work; he'll get us to think that we are different.

What are we to do? Submit ourselves to God and stand our ground. Insist that we belong to Christ and Satan has no authority over us. Pray a prayer of resistance.

Put on the Armor of God. If we are fighting a lion, we don't do it with bare hands. If we are up against tanks, a sling shot won't do.

God lists the pieces of spiritual armor needed to stand against the wiles of the devil. I'm glad He doesn't expect us to gain new territory, but simply to stand on the ground that Christ already conquered (Eph. 6:10–20).

We can't cover the pieces of armor in detail, but notice that they include honesty, righteousness, witnessing, faith, correct thinking, and the use of prayer and intercession. If any piece is missing, that's where we can expect an attack.

Remember that this battle is against spirits who are wicked, unprincipled, and destructive. They are by nature liars. If they tell the truth, it is only to deceive. They are mean, vicious, and bold. Don't expect them to give pleasure in sin without returning to collect.

Paul uses the expression, "in the heavenlies" five times in the Book of Ephesians. He uses the same expression in connection with our struggle, indicating that when we really become serious about our relationship with God, we're in for spiritual conflict. Satan would like us to fear him, so that we live wasted lives. It's even OK with him if we are moral, as long as we don't walk in the Spirit and bear the fruit that Christ promised we could. We must be sure that our armor is on.

Have a Ready Response to Satan. We have to tie all this information together so it can be used at a moment's notice. We may not have a half-hour's warning, for Satan can strike in seconds. I like what the Puritan writer Gibbon wrote about being prepared for the conflict:

> "Provide thyself with answers and retorts beforehand, against the subtle insinuations and delusions of thine enemy. For example: If Satan tells thee, as he often will, that the sin is pleasant, ask whether the grippings of conscience be so too, whether it be such a pleasant thing to be in hell, to be under the wrath of an Almighty Judge! If he tells thee, 'Nobody sees, thou mayest commit it safely,' ask whether he can put out God's all-seeing eye, whether he can find a place empty of the Divine presence

for thee to sin in, or whether he can blot out the items from the book of God's remembrance. . . . If he talks of prophets and earthly advantages that will accrue, ask what account it will turn to at the last day, and what profit there is if one should gain the whole world and lose his own soul, or what one should give in exchange for his soul! . . . When sin, like Jael, invites thee into her tent, with the lure and decoy of a lordly treatment, think of the nail and hammer which fastened Sisera dead to the ground" (John Gibbon, *Puritan Sermons,* Vol. 1, Richard Roberts Publishers, p. 98).

Paul warned, "I am afraid, lest as the serpent deceived Eve by his craftiness, your minds should be led astray from the simplicity and purity of devotion to Christ" (2 Cor. 11:3). We cannot let Satan have an advantage over us because we are ignorant of his devices.

See a Counselor. In some cases it is necessary to go to a pastor or Christian worker who has had experience in dealing with demonic warfare. Though Satan cannot possess Christians (possession implies an ownership that belongs to God alone), he can invade a life, particularly if we have opened the door to evil influences. The New Testament speaks of a person being "demonized," a specific harassment, and even the indwelling of the body. People who have given themselves over to Satan before they became Christians, or who have been in the occult, may need to confront wicked spirits directly. Even believers sometimes need demons expelled.

Satan's greatest weapon at this point is fear. He'll make you think that you are better off in your bondage than to go through the hassle of direct conflict. Don't believe it. He's afraid that his influence is soon to be over. He wants us to forget who we are in Christ, and settle for a life of failure. That's not the will of God, and it isn't necessary. The book, *The Adversary,* by Mark Bubeck has been of great help to many who need specific instruction on demonic deliverance.

As someone once said to me: "I couldn't shake myself free of immorality. I begged God to change me; I knew all the theology of victory, but it wouldn't work for me. No way. One day it came to a head. I was resisting a particular temptation for a half hour, but was overwhelmed by it. I was angry knowing that I would give in again. I called a Christian brother and shared honestly what was happening. Together we rebuked Satan, and after a time a great sense of peace came to me. It was so great to be free! That doesn't mean I'm not tempted anymore, but I know victory is possible."

Can you identify?

Study and Application

1. Memorize verses of Scripture to claim instantly in spiritual warfare (1 John 4:4; James 4:6–7; 1 Peter 5:8–9; Eph. 2:6).

2. After your past has been cleansed, learn to obey the first promptings of the Holy Spirit. The easiest time to resist temptation is the moment it comes to mind—it will never get easier. If necessary say, "Be gone Satan for it is written. . . ."; then quote verses of Scripture that you have memorized.

3. Ask God to show you excuses that you have used to indulge your mind or body in sensuality. Be sure that you have repented of these rationalizations.

4. Spend at least five minutes quoting Scripture before you fall asleep. This will cleanse your mind and guard it from wayward thoughts that often appear early in the morning.

5. Ponder Christ's words, "Go and sin no more lest a worse thing come unto thee" (John 5:14, KJV). What does this tell us about God's discipline for sinning flippantly?

6. Study the pieces of armor listed in Ephesians 6:10–20. What pieces do we tend to overlook? What can we do to wear this armor more consistently?

7. Learn to pray in warfare against Satan. For example, "Heavenly Father, I bow in worship and praise before You. I surrender myself completely and unreservedly to You. I take a stand against all the workings of Satan that would hinder me in this time of prayer, and I address myself only to the true and the living God and refuse any involvement of Satan in my prayer. . . ." Then praise God the Father, and affirm your position in Jesus Christ and put on the armor of God.

13

Emotional Healing

Sexual freedom is destroying the emotional stability of our society. One half of all divorces happen because one partner falls in love with someone who is more appealing. Given the frightening number of divorces, one half of all children born this year will be reared by a single parent at some point. Add to that 200,000 illegitimate births per year, and we can understand why millions of children are growing up feeling unwanted and emotionally rejected. In Vietnam, American servicemen fathered about 12,000 children who were considered outcasts because of their mixed blood. Many of them have starved to death, others live out in the streets and are treated like animals. Many children born in this country feel deep rejection—like the 15-year-old girl who was disowned by her parents. They gave away her clothes and sold her bicycle. They didn't want to hear from her again.

Abortion, which is a "mopping-up operation" that follows in the wake of the sexual revolution, attests to the fact that children are considered disposable, at the whim of the parents.

There are other hurts as well.

Girls who have been coaxed into bed by demanding boy-friends become resentful in marriage. Guilt and hostility cause frigidity and block the lines of communication. Impotency in men is usually traceable to promiscuity. Tens of thousands are angry because they've contracted a form of veneral disease from some partner they've trusted. They feel betrayed, vindictive.

The need for emotional healing multiplies each year as sexual looseness leaves its scars on the human psyche. When a child is unsure about whether he is wanted; or when a woman sees her husband transfer his affections to someone else, the human spirit is crushed. In fact, emotional pain is more difficult to accept than a physical disease. "The spirit of a man can endure his sickness, but a broken spirit, who can bear?" (Prov. 18:14)

Consider this story: A married woman in a moment of un-guarded passion had a sexual relationship with her husband's brother. Soon after she became pregnant, and for 20 years lived with the haunting suspicion that her husband may not be the biological father of their daughter.

When her husband was in a car accident, the whole family pulled together, hoping for his recovery. Months later he died, not knowing his wife's secret. After the funeral, the mother could bear the guilt no longer. Unfortunately, she told her daughter the whole story.

You can guess the effect this had on the girl. She's doing the whole scene—drugs, drink, illicit sex, and every form of perversion.

What caused this plunge into moral ruin? Her security (identi-ty) was taken from her in a single statement from her mother's lips. Her mother was now despised in her eyes. Her own origin was shrouded in uncertainty; she was bitter and didn't know who she really was.

Or consider the woman who gave birth to her father's child. One day her son found the family records and when he learned that his grandfather was his father, he committed suicide.

These two young people represent tens of thousands who are hostile toward their parents. The need to be loved and wanted is so great that when it is in doubt, the child cannot cope. Some people seek self-worth by pursuing promising sexual relationships. For example, a girl who doesn't have a strong loving father will crave the affection of a man who professes to love her. She'll sacrifice her virginity if that's the price she must pay, to establish self-esteem and a sense of belonging. When the relationship turns sour (as it must), her self-esteem is further destroyed. Then she's even worse off. Thus the cycle of insecurity is repeated. The next step may be drugs or alcohol. Many simply cannot handle the raw pain of rejection.

In a recent report on teenage alcoholism in Chicago, the bottom line was that the young people of today are so insecure because of the breakup of the home, that they cannot tolerate the emptiness they feel. They turn to alcohol to deaden the emotional pain.

Given the hard facts of illegitimacy, incest, child abuse, and parental failure, can a person be put back together emotionally? Can an identity be firmly established independently of the nuclear family?

Here are some starting points toward emotional wholeness.

Forgive Those Who Have Wronged Us

It's difficult, but its possible. Though every fiber of your body revolts against forgiving your parents, husband, or boyfriend, it must be done. Bitterness will never change the past; it will not bring the adversary to his knees in humble confession. Chances are the person who has wronged you couldn't care less about how you're feeling. Sin dulls the senses, it deadens the most elementary spark of human decency and kindness. A person who has sinned sexually and then tried to take care of that blotch on his own (without casting himself upon the mercy of God) is capable of every form of verbal and physical cruelty. We read of those who are ignorant and have "become calloused, have given themselves over to sensuality, for the practice of every kind of impurity with greediness" (Eph. 4:19). Again, Paul speaks of those who are "seared in their own conscience as with a branding iron" (1 Tim. 4:2).

This explains why a father who leaves his family can ignore the feelings of his children. They may cry out to him for recognition and acceptance, but he won't even send them a birthday card. I've known children to weep, hoping that their fathers will love them, but such fathers are too selfish to see beyond their own biological needs. In a word, a person who gives himself to sensuality is reduced to an animal. Only what he sees, thinks, and feels matters; the feelings of others are irrelevant.

Such people seldom admit their failures and ask for forgiveness. God alone can bring them to their senses. Apart from a miracle, their hearts of stone will never be exchanged for hearts of flesh (Ezek. 11:19).

So we must forgive those who have wronged us even if they never ask for forgiveness; chances are they won't. In such cases, forgiveness is primarily an act done for our own good. Hostility will ruin any chance for emotional wholeness.

How can we forgive? By reminding ourselves how much God has forgiven us. That's the standard of the New Testament "Forgiving each other, just as God in Christ has also forgiven you" (Eph. 4:32). Forgive whether we feel like it or not. It's a choice we make regardless of how painful it becomes.

And if the bitterness lingers? We must reject it in Christ's name. In faith affirm our trust in the promises of God. We might want to even the score, but that's God's responsibility. "Never take your own revenge, beloved, but leave room for the wrath of God, for it is written, 'Vengeance is Mine, I will repay, says the Lord' " (Rom. 12:19).

How does a husband forgive his wife for committing adultery? One woman was involved in such an affair two years ago.

Ever since she was married she regretted that she had not dated a certain man whom she found to be sexually attractive. The seed of thought grew until she had a chance to act out her fantasies.

For two years she lived with the knowledge that she had betrayed her husband. Through repentance she successfully dealt with feelings of guilt and shame, but she felt that one more step had to be taken. She had to tell her husband what had happened. He reacted angrily and was emotionally devastated. He couldn't believe that such a thing could happen to a couple that had been happily married for 10 years. Now he has rejected his wife. There's virtually no verbal communication and no sexual relationship.

It would be easy to say that the wife made a mistake in sharing this secret with him. Whether it was wise or foolish is difficult to say, but God can use this experience in their marriage, if each responds correctly.

Since the wife has repented, how should the husband respond? Fortunately, God doesn't withhold forgiveness and neither should we. To say that what happened is unfair, is true, but beside the point. Very few happenings in life are fair. In fact, little happened in Christ's life that was fair.

The Prophet Hosea, at God's instruction, married a woman named Gomer. She was an adulteress, and even had a child by one of her lovers, hence his name, Lo-Ammi (meaning "not my people"). Then she became a prostitute, flitting from one man to another. Yet the prophet waited for her return and even bought her at a slave auction when her life of sin had run its course. The prediction for Gomer and Israel had been, "I will betroth you to Me forever; yes, I will betroth you to Me in righteousness and in justice, in loving-kindness and in compassion, and I will betroth you to Me in faithfulness. Then you will know the Lord" (Hosea 2:19–20).

Clearly, she was fully restored and even regarded as a pure

woman again. In fact, "She will sing there as in the days of her youth" says the prophet (2:15). The bird with a broken wing soars once again. Jesus reserves harsh judgment for those who refuse to be as gracious in their forgiveness as God is in His. The forgiven servant who would not forgive his fellow servant was handed over to the torturers until he should repay all that was owed by him. Then Christ adds, "So shall My heavenly Father also do to you, if each of you does not forgive his brother from your heart" (Matt. 18:35). Of course a man can forgive his wife, and their marriage can be beautifully restored. Such a shattering experience need not be the end of their dreams.

Deborah Roberts, a Christian girl who was raped while doing visitation for a church on Chicago's south side, learned that wholeness comes by feeling worthy and valuable again. She had lost her virginity and with it her self-respect. How could she forgive the rapist? She knew that the feelings of guilt and shame she had would never leave her unless she was prepared to forgive. After months of hurt, she concluded, "No one should ever be given the privilege of robbing someone else of his sense of dignity. What I mean is this: If you live perpetually with a sense of guilt and shame because of someone else's sin, you are really letting them control you. What a tragedy if Roger Gray had permanent control over the life of Deborah Roberts and she would not have been able to rebuild herself" (*Raped,* Zondervan, p. 133).

Do you really want your parents, wife, or husband to control you? Do you really want them to dictate how you will feel and determine the degree of your bitterness? You must choose to forgive if for no other reason, you deserve it yourself. In Christ's name, choose to forgive.

Forgive God
Forgiving people is one thing, but what about God? Is He not the sovereign Lord of the universe? Job railed against God

because he didn't die in the womb; that would have been better than the tragedies that he was expected to accept.

God could have banished Satan to another planet, created a man who would choose to obey Him. "Where was He when my father and brother raped me at the age of 10?" a young woman in her 20s asked with bitterness. "What kind of a God is He if He watched without doing anything?"

That's exactly the same question Deborah Roberts faced. After reading Psalm 121 with its great promises of God's keeping power and guidance in the life of a Christian, Deborah asked, "What about that, God? Shouldn't I believe Your promises? I thought I was special to You. Did I read that wrong or wasn't that a promise from You to protect me? I just don't understand. Are You a loving God or are you a vengeful God? Do You have a reason for me to be raped? Did you really want that to happen to me? What reason could be good enough for that kind of pain? I nearly killed myself over it. Do You remember that?" (*Raped,* p. 128)

Her ultimate conclusion is the one we are forced to accept: God's love does not prevent us from the tragedies of sexual abuse or any other kind of mistreatment. Christ was God's "beloved Son" yet the Father didn't shield Him from the torture of crucifixion. That crime, despite its horror, has become for us a fountain of blessing. The horror of Good Friday must be understood in the light of the joy of Easter Sunday.

God can do the same with the ugly hurts of life. Jephthah was an illegitimate child, yet God used Him mightily (Jud. 11:1, 29, 32). Rahab was a prostitute, but became a special heroine of faith (Heb. 11:31).

When you become angry with God, you're actually trading places with Him. You are trying to become greater than He by bringing Him into your law court and putting Him on trial. William Cowper spoke of those who wished to indict God. They:

> Snatch from God's hand
> The balance and the rod,
> Rejudge His justice
> And be the judge of God.

Confess the bitterness you have toward Him. Concentrate on His infinite grace and be forgiven and accepted.

Someone has said that God can put anyone back together, as long as we give Him all the pieces. Bitterness must be surrendered.

See Yourself as Valuable to God

Self-hatred is one of the devil's most effective weapons. When we reject ourselves, we are demeaning the highest order of God's earthly creation.

Those who have been mistreated often blame themselves for their lot in life, even though they may be the victims of other people's sins. Children of divorced parents may think they were the cause of the split; a child forced into an incestuous relationship feels dirty; and a girl raped by a sexual maniac is overcome by self-contempt. False guilt is just as devastating as real guilt if not resolved.

God wants us to feel good about ourselves. That is, we must thank Him that we were created by Him and be satisfied with the way we look. What is more, we must accept our circumstances as a part of a plan out of which God wants to display His mercy and loving-kindness.

Read the Book of Ephesians, jotting down all of the descriptive terms that apply to us as God's people. We were chosen in Christ before the foundation of the world, adopted, accepted, redeemed from sin's power, and have received the gift of the Holy Spirit. We have become heirs of God and joint heirs with Christ. If the value of an object is dependent on the price paid for it, we rate highly, for we were purchased at high cost (1 Peter 1:18–19). Consequently, our body now belongs to God (1 Cor. 6:19–20).

Even our physical characteristics are God ordained. David wrote that God meticulously plans the features of the unborn (Ps. 139:13–16). Remember that before we were born God called us by name and conferred on us the special privilege of being one of His children.

Emotional healing takes time, but the pace is quickened when we accept forgiveness and cleansing, and then affirm with the Scriptures that we are number one on God's list of priorities in the universe.

Share Your Struggles

Have you ever wondered why facts sometimes don't work in and of themselves? Those of us who believe in biblical counseling sometimes fall into the trap of thinking that the antidote to every problem is information, that the truths of the Scripture must simply be memorized and applied.

Not so.

Relationships are sometimes the key to overcoming personal battles. Just yesterday a man shared secret struggles he had never been able to articulate before. When he was finished, I gave him a few suggestions, but they were not nearly as important as the fact that he had been able to share his inner self with another human being. It was a relief for him to be able to share openly and yet be affirmed and accepted.

We derive the answer to the question "Who am I?" from other people. That's why parents play such a crucial role in helping a child establish his identity. But if they fail, the body of Christ has the responsibility of supplying the emotional reinforcements so necessary for healing. We are after all, the continuation of Christ's ministry on earth. Christ is physically present on earth through us.

One woman was so filled with self-hatred that she couldn't look at herself in the mirror. She'd just part her hair out of the corner of her eye never seeing herself directly. What changed her? Someone told her that she was loved and accepted. Then she was hugged, and made to feel she was a worthy human being. We'll never know how many emotional problems would be solved if we all exercised the tenderness and concern of Christ our Saviour.

Who Are You?

A Lutheran minister told seminary students that they'd be less likely to fall into moral temptation if they wore their clerical garb. He understood that our perception of ourselves determines how we act.

How do you perceive yourself? If the answer is bitter, angry, guilty, or any other negative adjective, you will steadily slide back into a moral swamp. You will have no reason to look up, no plans to move to higher ground. Your negative thoughts will work themselves into the common habits of everyday life.

Or are you willing to see yourself in a different perspective? Even if you don't feel loved and accepted are you willing to take it by faith? God has painted a portrait of you that is quite different from the one you may have of yourself. He's able to change the way you see yourself, and thereby change your behavior and feelings.

We read of several in the Bible who experienced identity crises. Moses asked God, "Who am I?" God didn't answer his question directly; rather He said, "I am who I am" (Ex. 3:14). Then God asked him to tell the sons of Israel, "I Am has sent me" (3:14). Moses learned that his self-identity could only be understood with reference to his relationship with God. It really didn't matter who Moses was, as long as Moses knew who God was and was obedient to His will.

Sometimes God actually changed a person's name to give him a new reputation to look up to. God was communicating His confidence that special blessings lay ahead.

Abram meaning "high father" becomes Abraham "the father of many nations."

Jacob which means "cheater" becomes Israel "a prince of God."

Simon possibly a derivative of Simeon which means "hearing" is renamed Peter "the rock."

Now it's your turn. What is your name? Is it guilt, anger, sensuality? God wants to give you a new name that identifies you as His special child. To those who overcome He says, "I will give him a white stone, and a new name written on the stone, which no one knows but he who receives it" (Rev. 2:17).

With your past behind you, and your future in God's hands, you can be emotionally whole.

Study and Application

1. What kind of childhood experiences erode self-esteem? What responsibilities do parents have in developing self-esteem?

2. How did Christ deal with a woman caught in shame and guilt? (John 8:1–11) What lessons are in this for us?

3. What is the responsibility of the body of Christ toward one another in times of emotional need? Study passages such as Romans 12:5; 14:1–4, 1 Corinthians 12:26–27, Galatians 6:1–5.

4. How did Christ use Peter's failures to develop him? Study passages such as, Matthew 14:28–31, 16:16–23, 18:21–22, Luke 5:8–10, 22:31–32, John 6:66–68, 13:1–14, 18:10–11.

5. How does being accepted in Christ provide the foundation for accepting others? (Eph. 1:6)

14

Facing Tomorrow

Where do you go from here? Information is of no help unless you are ready to apply it when you need it.

Suppose you lived in a city that was continually under attack. An enemy would harass the inhabitants, leave, and return through the same hole in the wall. Don't you think that the citizens would devise a strategy for defense?

Some of us succumb to the same sins again and again yet we don't take time to "close the hole in the wall."

For most of us, our walk with God is a mixed bag. Times of victory are interspersed with times of defeat. The preparations we make during the good times will determine our responses when the temptations come.

Since the mind is the primary battleground, you must guard it carefully by being alert to sinful fantasies and rationalizations.

> My soul, be on thy guard
> Ten thousand foes arise
> A host of sins are pressing hard
> To draw thee from the skies.

Do you know precisely what you will do when sensuality comes into your life? Let me encourage you to take time to devise your strategy for that inevitable confrontation.

Begin by sharing your struggle with one or two people whom you trust. You'll be strengthened by their prayerful support and God will use this act of humility in your life. To admit a need to others is proof that you've come to the end of your own resources. It means that you are more concerned about overcoming your sin, than you are about what people may think.

No Substitute for Submitting

Repentance begins as an act, but must continue as an attitude. We must be willing to accept whatever God brings into our lives. There is no substitute for submitting fully to God before 9 every morning. Don't think that prayer is just talking to God; it's also waiting in quietness, asking Him to show us where we are out of agreement with Him.

Stay current with God on every single issue. Don't let "weeds" (stray thought) begin to accumulate or they will become firmly rooted again. If you've got to pray 10 times a day, do it, but stay in fellowship with God whatever the cost.

Meditate on the Scriptures

The Word of God is a cleansing agent. "You are already clean because of the Word which I have spoken to you" (John 15:3). It also fortifies us against sin. "How can a young man keep his way pure? By keeping it according to Thy Word" (Ps. 119:9).

We can unleash the power of God's Word by reading the Scripture every day and writing down in a notebook what we observed in a passage. Nothing can take the place of God's Word occupying our minds. We can memorize verses of Scripture directly related to areas of temptation, and use them at a moment's notice. When temptation comes, we can say, "I resist that temptation in Jesus' name," and quote the verses we've learned.

One man repeated the verse, "Blessed are the pure in heart, for they shall see God" (Matt. 5:8) five times the moment he was confronted with sensual thoughts. *Then* he was able to say *no* to lust and *yes* to God.

Every Temptation Is a Stepping Stone

You're struggling? We all are, but we have an opportunity to prove that Christ is stronger than the flesh. God is using our trials to sift through our lives to separate the temporal from the eternal. He's asking: "Are you willing to give up the cherished pleasures of the heart in favor of fellowship with Me?"

Thank God for temptation. We are answerable to Him, and He has allowed testing in our lives because He has lessons to teach us. An attitude of praise for the thorn in the flesh will give God a chance to make His strength perfect in weakness. Memorize psalms of praise to God and concentrate on becoming a worshiper.

Never give up. Every failure brings us to a point of fuller surrender to God. We learn that sin is evil and God is righteous. We repent more deeply each time until God brings us to helplessness. The clay totally submits to the Potter.

You should work out the details of your own plan. Know precisely what you will do when temptation comes. Come to the battle prepared—ready for emergencies.

"If you abide in Me and My Word, then you are truly disciples of Mine; and you shall know the truth, and the truth shall make you free" (John 8:31–32).

"If therefore the Son shall make you free, you shall be free indeed" (v. 36).

Other Books by Erwin Lutzer:

How to Say No to a Stubborn Habit
Every day you face the oldest human dilemma—the choice between good and evil. The good news is that you can say No to sin and Yes to God.

Managing Your Emotions
This book will help you cope with feelings that may be out of control. See why only God can completely heal your emotional wounds and put you back on the road to emotional wholeness.

When a Good Man Falls
Can a Christian hope to become effective again after being tripped up by sin? Discover how to make a comeback—or how to help a loved one recover from seeming ruin.